PRAISE FOR *BAMBOO STRONG*

'This book cuts to the chase as to why business owners and executives fail in new markets and cultures. It provides deep insights into the global challenges businesses face and delivers practical and innovative sol·
immediately. It's de:
handbook of the dec:

Jason Jennings,
of *The High Speed Company, The Reinventors, Less Is More*, and *Think BIG—Act Small*

'An essential read that is a wise and powerful compendium of strategies to help you truly prosper as a business owner or executive in the new global economy. *Bamboo Strong* is about the most important problems arising today in the global economy, and it proposes strategies companies can implement now for a more fruitful tomorrow!'

Marshall Goldsmith, author of the #1 *New York Times* bestseller, *Triggers*

'A must-read for anyone who owns or manages a multicultural organisation or business and wants to create a culture of creativity and innovation based on diversity.'

John Mattone, the world's #1 authority on leadership and culture

'David is a very rare and special talent, and as with all those who were born to make a difference to our world, he openly shares his learning, insights, and experiences for our betterment. *Bamboo Strong* is a beautiful creation that is a book for the times we live in today and a guide for the world we would like to live in tomorrow. It challenged me and argued with me, made me laugh out loud, and made me weep with both joy and hurt. But, just like the bamboo in the title, it was supple enough to bend and accommodate my diversity and difference, and it was also strong enough to guide me when I wandered off near danger. A book for everyone and anyone you care about. An essential guide for the times we live in.'

René Carayol, MBE, CEO,
Inspired Leaders Network

'In his fascinating, beautifully written, and page-turning book, David helps you to uncover the essential skills you need to influence and inspire others who come from cultures that are not your own. In an era when the world has become a village and businesses of almost every kind operate in global markets, it has never been more important to acquire these lessons. Lean in to learn from a wonderful array of knowledge, expertise, and personal stories that will assuredly help you to chart a course to masterful cross-cultural communication.'

Eamonn O'Brien, founder of The
Reluctant Speakers Club and author of
How to Make Powerful Speeches

'This is the beautifully written and fascinating tale of David's journey to becoming a global citizen. Rather than boring you with classroom theory, you'll be enlightened and inspired to accompany him on his travels to embrace cultural intelligence so that you too can become a more effective leader in this new global world. For any business or organisation looking to forge profitable and peaceful partnerships across borders, I highly recommend you read this book and learn from David who is a visionary leader for the twenty-first century.'

Rachel Henke, International Freedom Coach and bestselling author of *The Freedom Solution*

'With his invaluable insights and cultural intelligence practices, David has opened a new door for global business travellers. The *Bamboo Strong* mindset and David's newly designed dynamic activities are created to challenge thinking, encourage flexibility, and catalyze self-discovery. The flexible nature of this new guide is quintessentially bamboo: encouraging readers to nurture their own journey of self-discovery while cultivating the resilience to thrive in the complex circumstances and rich cultures of our time.'

Sharon Schweitzer, JD, President, Protocol & Etiquette Worldwide, LLC, and author of the *Access to Asia: Your Multicultural Business Guides* series

'For anyone planning to engage with other countries, whether in business or out of a sense of adventure, this is an invaluable work. In today's fast-moving and constantly changing world, *Bamboo Strong* provides the navigational chart to ensure smooth sailing in the complex waters of other cultures. It gives helpful insights through a rich array of anecdotes and stories to assist those seeking a greater understanding of sometimes seemingly confusing situations. An invaluable addition to anyone's armoury of cross-cultural knowledge!'

Roddy Gow, Chairman and founder, Asia Scotland Institute

'*Bamboo Strong* is a must-read for those who live in a culturally diversified environment, be it in the physical or online world. In this innovative and yet practical book, David educates and inspires readers with his authentic personal stories, third-party evidence and research, and a high CQ sense of humour that can resonate and connect with each of us, regardless of our skin colour and life experience. This is a great read for both business and leisure in the new global economy.'

Sally Maier-Yip, Managing Director, 11K Consulting

'*Bamboo Strong* should be essential reading for anyone hoping to be successful in business. The central message of this book is that unless you are open to the challenges of cultural intelligence (understanding the language within the language) you will not succeed. Bamboo is used as a good example of the need for malleability, as it has the ability to bend and accommodate in stressful conditions without losing its original shape. Recognizing that we live and work in a modern global village, companies are choosing to become matrix organizations and to embrace diversity as an opportunity in the search for talent. To win this talent race, an increasing number of successful companies are investing in understanding the implications of cultural intelligence.'

Mariano A. Davies, President and CEO,
British Chamber of Commerce in Denmark

'Global executives need cross-cultural skills and intelligence now more than ever before. Success and the ability to out-perform your competitors in international markets require sensitivity towards diverse local cultures and business etiquette. *Bamboo Strong* will guide you on this path, its gift being not only the enrichment of your business but also an enrichment of your life experience. A wonderful read packed with insights and examples to build awareness and provide the skills necessary to perform effectively across markets. This book will equip you to achieve a level of intercultural intelligence that is critical to long-term success in the global workplace. So take up the challenge and dive in!'

Catherine Lai, CEO,
Albest International Limited

'Cultural intelligence is probably the most important skill required by today's leaders. In this masterful and incisive book, David demonstrates why and how to become more resilient and flexible, for greater success in cross-cultural relationships.'

Mindy Gibbins-Klein, MBA, international speaker and author of *The Thoughtful Leader*

'At long last, a book that explodes the myth that many businesses hold about culture being associated with optional skills on the peripheries of business but instead reveals how a high level of CQ impacts directly on profitability and performance for global businesses. Using personal experiences combined with proven academic studies, David celebrates the importance of cross-cultural effectiveness as a must-have skill for today's global managers, especially in today's evolving and multicultural world, where mastery of these skills can mean the difference between a project's success or failure.'

Sarah Parsons, Managing Director, Japan in Perspective

'The level of success in today's globalized commerce strongly depends on the cultural intelligence of leaders, which cannot be gained without sophisticated knowledge. *Bamboo Strong* explains this complex phenomenon in a very classy, elegant, and practical manner.'

Dr. Oleg Konovalov, DBA, MBA, author of *Organisational Anatomy*

'You are at the center of the global experience. How can you become a Bamboo Leader? You will need your own copy of *Bamboo Strong* to understand the analogy. You will also need to be open to the experience and ready to travel. You will want to discover and develop that part of your brain (or heart) that is like your cultural muscle. *Bamboo Strong* is not a list of facts or behaviors that are acceptable or best avoided. It is a very personal and experiential book about life, courage, and resilience. It raises awareness of cultural intelligence and introduces new ways of looking at diversity, so that we can all identify and think of our own circumstances and stories.'

Sophie Leroi, Executive and Global Leadership Coach, founder, The Focus Room, LLC

'We are crossing borders and bridging worlds now faster than ever before. This timely book is a powerful tool that lets us ride on the evolutionary wave towards becoming a flexible Bamboo Leader and bridges the separations that we see outside ourselves so we can do better business. David guides us to work with our inner separations, which are at the root of almost all the pains and problems we experience in daily life. This is a book with a heart and sense of balance that I consider rare at this level of business books. David's message helps us lower our own barriers to become more responsive, share, grow, and profit together.'

Adam Frewer, global healer, channel, and author of *From Baggage to Balance*

PRAISE FOR *THE AGE OF PLURALISM*

'Here is a superb resource for any leader, executive or coach who wants to quickly rise to a new level of success in the complex and richly diverse business world of today and tomorrow.'

Marshall Goldsmith, *Thinkers 50 –*
World's Most Influential Leadership
Thinker (only 2 x winner)

If you want to succeed in the global marketplace, and to lead more collaborative, high performing teams at home and overseas, this is the book for you.'

John Mattone, the number one
authority on Intelligent Leadership and
the world's top executive coach

'*The Age of Pluralism* is a highly engaging read for global companies, leaders and high-performing teams. Written with a rare combination of personal narrative, humour and 21-century tools for strengthening leadership agility, this is very much a book for our rapidly changing times. I would recommend it as essential reading for all current and emerging leaders as well as their coaches.'

Dr. Thomas D. Zweifel, award-winning
author of *Culture Clash 2: Managing
the Global High-Performance Team*

'As somebody born in Argentina, who has lived in the USA and is now a British citizen, David's book strikes a chord. I consider myself both Argentine and British, and have embraced aspects of both cultures. In this sense, I'm a hybrid. In my leadership development work across the world, I see the pluralism David talks about manifested in how leaders navigate uncertainty, connect people and ideas, and deliver strategy through others. A very worthwhile read for any global citizen, senior leader or human resources leader who wants to go beyond diversity and cultural awareness.'

Mariano Tufro, Director, Leadership Minds Ltd.

'The *Age of Pluralism* goes directly to the heart of why current and emerging leaders fail to make the progress they want in our increasingly diverse world. The author provides deep insights into the challenges we face, and proposes practical and innovative solutions you can profit from for years to come.'

Tony J. Selimi, international number one best-selling author of *A Path to Wisdom*

'The days of states in the global community existing within a singular cultural concept are long past. In the current framework of the global economy, we are becoming increasingly aware of the need to be more inclusive of the diversity that our global communities generate. Leadership as a whole is facing new challenges that past leadership did not encounter, at least not to the levels we are witnessing today.

The Age of Pluralism is a striking and timely reminder of the threats that exist for our emerging leaders. At the very moment when there is a clear and pressing need to prepare our leaders for the challenges of tomorrow, they find themselves seriously undervalued by senior leadership. David Clive Price showcases the reality facing our current leadership teams across the world. He explores the ever-present need for organisations to utilize the tools found in executive coaching to help their current emerging and high-potential leaders to succeed in positions of increasing seniority and responsibility.'

Curtis Smith, Founder & CEO,
Thee Executive-Panel, LLC

'In The Age of Pluralism, David Clive Price explores the increasing diversity of our times, and how we can harness the forces of pluralism to create more human centric leaders. By addressing the leadership gap between performance and coaching, David offers invaluable tools and resources as well as documented cases to accompany his personal, authentic narrative. A brilliant piece of work and highly relevant to today's global culture.'

Vivien Hunt, Leadership Coach and
Director, Lead Source Coaching

'The Age of Pluralism distils a wealth of knowledge, real-life case studies and personal experiences from around the globe to produce an invaluable guide for both the next generation of future leaders and experienced executives alike.'

Grant Hall, Founder and CEO,
League Cultural Diplomacy

BAMBOO
STRONG

BAMBOO STRONG

CULTURAL INTELLIGENCE SECRETS TO SUCCEED IN THE NEW GLOBAL ECONOMY

DAVID CLIVE PRICE

WILDBLUE
PRESS

WildBluePress.com

BAMBOO STRONG published by:

WILDBLUE PRESS
P.O. Box 102440
Denver, Colorado 80250

Publisher Disclaimer: Any opinions, statements of fact or fiction, descriptions, dialogue, and citations found in this book were provided by the author, and are solely those of the author. The publisher makes no claim as to their veracity or accuracy, and assumes no liability for the content.

WILDBLUE PRESS is registered at the U.S. Patent and Trademark Offices.

ISBN 978-1-947290-91-4 Trade Paperback
ISBN 978-1-947290-90-7 eBook

Interior Formatting/Book Cover Design by Elijah Toten
www.totencreative.com

For Simon, Shiu Ming
My cross-cultural mentor

'Bamboo is flexible, bending with the wind but never breaking, capable of adapting to any circumstance. It suggests resilience, meaning that we have the ability to bounce back even from the most difficult times. Your ability to thrive depends, in the end, on your attitude to your life circumstances. Take everything in your stride with grace, putting forth energy when it is needed, yet always staying calm inwardly.'

Ping Fu, *Bend, Not Break*

CONTENTS

FOREWORD

It is my belief that the major challenge for most executives isn't failing to understand the practice of leadership, it is practising their understanding of leadership. This is not a book about leadership theory or philosophy; although it is backed up by proven scholarly research. It is about leadership in action.

We are living in an age when our workgroups are more diverse than ever before, and there is an increasing need for flexible global leadership across borders and cultures. This book focuses on *you*, on what you can do to develop and adapt your behaviour for all cross-cultural situations.

It provides guidance, insights, and personal examples to motivate, inspire, and reward you by taking specific actions to develop your cultural intelligence. However, this is not a book you can skim through hoping to pick up a few pointers. The perspectives it offers are incremental; the vision it presents grows broader and deeper the more you read.

David shows us that to become successful Bamboo Leaders we must develop both resilience and flexibility, just like the bamboo bends with the wind but is rooted in strength. Transformation is achieved through daily practice, discipline, and, above all, by embracing diversity in our daily actions without losing our authenticity.

The book's theme resonates strongly with me. Cross-cultural confidence and sophistication are fast becoming life skills that global CEOs and their senior teams neglect at their peril. Even organizations that don't operate internationally can benefit from a culturally intelligent strategy for diverse workforces, generations, geographies, and functions. If you want to succeed in the global marketplace and to lead more effective, high-performing teams at home, this is the book for you.

Marshall Goldsmith
International bestselling author and editor
of 35 books including *What Got You Here Won't Get You There* and *Triggers*

ACKNOWLEDGEMENTS

I was inspired to write *Bamboo Strong* above all by my extraordinary clients, readers, online community, friends, and cross-cultural explorers all over the world. Your examples, questions, and stories continued to drive me on to fresh discoveries and new visions just when it seemed my own stock of cultural intelligence lessons might be running low.

There are many people in many countries who have helped and mentored me, taken me under their wing, and revealed to me the wonders, excitement, and unexpected vistas of living and working in new cultures and environments. They know who they are, and I thank them for their tolerance, kindness, and love.

I'd like to thank John Eggen and his team at Mission Publishing for supporting me through the creative stages of this book and helping me bring its systems and teachings out into the world.

I'd also like to thank the wonderful team at Wildblue Press as well as Anne Carley, Stephanie Lawyer, Kimb Manson, and Charlotte Mouncey, who made the book possible, Rachel Henke for her inspirational coaching, Hugh Culver for sharing with me his secrets to international speaking, and Devorah Spilman for helping me recreate and test my most soul-searching stories.

And finally thank you to my dear, supportive husband, Simon, who continues to believe in me regardless and has always supported me in my passion to make the world a better place. I love and cherish you.

AUTHOR'S NOTE

Diversity is the new normal and we'd better get used to it.

We are living and working in an age of rapid change: increasing globalisation and connectivity, faster time to market, more cross-border mergers and acquisitions, many new and more accessible markets, and greater mobility of work-forces and teams. Even thirty years ago, we would have been able to more or less predict whom our business partners, suppliers, distributors, customers, bosses, work colleagues, and team members would be. We would have expected to interact with them safe in the certainty that most of them would be People Like Us.

Nowadays, these certainties are gone. Under the impact of migration, globalisation, and the concentration of work in super-connected cities across the world, we are dealing with people of many different national, ethnic, cultural, social, and generational backgrounds on a daily basis.

This means we are now required to develop and use a once neglected skill—cultural intelligence—as never before. The good news is that cultural intelligence can be discovered and forged into a powerful capability for success in the new global economy. Two decades of research by scholars in dozens of countries have contributed to the evolution of the cultural intelligence (CQ)* model, a simple and clear four-part system for approaching culturally diverse situations and the challenges of cross-cultural encounters.

I have written this book as a very personal exploration

of the CQ model and its four capabilities—CQ Drive, CQ Knowledge, CQ Strategy, and CQ Action. Each of the central chapters takes as its reference point one of the four aspects of the CQ model as laid out in the excellent studies and publications of the Cultural Intelligence Center, LLC, based in Grand Rapids, Michigan.

But I also believe that, beyond the systematic application and development of cultural intelligence, the real driver for success in today's globalized world is you. In other words, it's your own pliancy, adaptability, readiness to learn and to empathize. Cultural intelligence starts with the personal— with how you see yourself in different cultural situations, how much awareness you have of your own culture, and how it affects your thinking and behaviour.

This book is intended to both motivate and inspire you rather than dull you with facts or extensive lists of behaviour. Throughout my life, I've been very fortunate and privileged to travel, live, and work in many countries around the globe.

I've married into families from two cultures that are very different to my own. I've had a rich variety of diverse occupations from academic to wine and olive farmer, to novelist, travel writer, international speechwriter and speaker, cross-cultural mentor, business guide, and strategist. But this does not necessarily make me unique. The fact is, many of us are now global citizens of a world where multicultural diversity exists right on our doorstep and in all aspects of our lives, from going to the gym to shopping to dining out to using social media.

I didn't start off as a global citizen. I grew up in a very different environment of People Like Us, of safe certainties, of expected behaviour and social assumptions that were typical of an Anglo-Welsh, London-born, grammar school- and university-educated boy of the time. It was only when

I broke away from this background, and went to live with my first husband in Switzerland and Italy, that I discovered the elements of cultural intelligence that were to stand me in such good stead in my future life and career.

One of the central themes of this book is that you can only develop strong cultural intelligence if you are open to, and ready to learn from, cross-cultural experiences in real life. And the more of them you experience, the stronger your CQ will be.

I have made countless cultural mistakes and blunders in new cultural environments and when meeting new people from other backgrounds and countries. However, I have never allowed them to deter me from taking a risk, trying things out, stepping into the dark. The various stages of the cultural intelligence journey I guide you through in this book—Innovation, Courage, Exploration, Perspective, Performance, and Transformation—are intended as stepping-stones into this new world I discovered, a world of cross-cultural adventure, wonder, and celebration.

Much of the guidance I offer is personal, but I also walk you through strategies and techniques to move you forward on your CQ journey. For this reason, at the end of each chapter there is a link to a Cultural Intelligence (CQ) Planner on my website: www.davidcliveprice.com/planner.

This Cultural Intelligence (CQ) Planner can provide you or your organisation with the essential skills to become a confident participant in cross-cultural encounters. It includes a summary of the action points of that particular section, so that you can create your own cultural intelligence strategy as you move onwards in your journey from Courage to Transformation.

The Cultural Intelligence (CQ) Planner also includes a grid of the four CQ capabilities; a number of assessment tools to determine your own and your colleagues' cultural profiles; multiple-choice questions to explore the cultural profiles of a variety of countries; a step-by-step builder to develop your organisation's cultural intelligence strategy; and checklists and tips.

Together with the mentoring programs laid out at the back of the book, the Cultural Intelligence (CQ) Planner is intended to provide you with all the help you need to become a confident participant in cross-cultural encounters and to build relationships, communicate, negotiate, and lead across cultures both at home and overseas—in other words, to become what I call a true Bamboo Leader.

I have taken this term, and the title of this book, *Bamboo Strong*, from the giant, woody grass that grows and transforms so rapidly when it is cut down. Bamboo easily withstands the harshness of winter. It is incredibly strong and yet flexes and bends with the force of the wind or rain. That is why the ancient Chinese regarded the bamboo as a symbol of strength, courage, and resilience.

Cultural intelligence work is often complex and challenging. It requires patience, and nuance, and subtlety, which is perhaps why, according to research carried out by Dr David Livermore of the Cultural Intelligence Center, more than 90 percent of global executives identify cross-cultural effectiveness as their biggest challenge. If you have a black-and-white view of the world and of cultural issues, if you are impatient in new situations and fearful of losing control, cultural intelligence might not be for you. However, if you can train yourself to develop your CQ, you stand a much greater chance of success in today's global economy.

This essential capability is in even greater demand in a time of mass migration, religious fundamentalism, and a ready recourse to xenophobia and political demagoguery.

The world needs leaders with high CQ—not only to spread the message of tolerance but also to provide deeper and more nuanced insights into other viewpoints, conflicting opinions, and unfamiliar traditions and beliefs. It's easy to fall back on stereotype and intolerance.

This book suggests there is another way. It's a path of excitement and curiosity, of surprise and sheer delight in the discovery of other approaches and other viewpoints. I still feel thrilled when I set out in a new city in an unfamiliar country, and I know that my cultural intelligence will guide me on my progress to new experiences and world views, to new friends and new pastures.

I hope that this book will encourage you to undertake a similar journey of transformation based on a growing ability to flex with the winds of new experiences, different ways of thinking, and unfamiliar beliefs. In our drive to become true Bamboo Leaders, we should take heart. We are not showing weakness. We are helping to make the world a better place. Please let me know about your cross-cultural experiences. You can connect with me by registering for the complimentary Cultural Intelligence (CQ)* Planner and joining my email subscriber list.

You can also reach out to me on social media and read about my Bamboo Strong™ strategies and discoveries at http://www.davidcliveprice.com

To your successful CQ journey!

Dr David Clive Price
Global Executive Coach
Author of *The Age of Pluralism*

---

*CQ® is a registered trademark of the Cultural Intelligence Center, LLC

INNOVATION

THE WORLD IS FLAT—OR IS IT?

I was sitting in the lobby of the Grand Hotel in Montreux, Switzerland, when Vladimir Nabokov walked in and sat down almost opposite me.

I knew it was the world-famous novelist because David nudged me and whispered his name. Once I was alerted, I could recognize the domed forehead and huge eyes, the liver spots on his cheek, the suit with the wide lapels from the dust jacket of *Ada*, which I'd recently read with rapt attention for all of its eight hundred or so pages.

So, there we sat on a narrow bench, two star-truck fans in their mid-twenties, watching a cultural icon of the twentieth century casually looking through a local newspaper. And suddenly I dropped my most recent read, a novel by Patricia Highsmith. For a moment, there was no reaction from Nabokov. But then I saw those huge eyes swivel in our direction. He didn't look at me, at least not at first. He looked at the book and the book's title—*Ripley's Game*— and for a second those eyes seemed to narrow in amusement. There was a twinkle there. Finally, he straightened, looked directly at me, and half smiled, questioning with his head whether I was going to pick the book up.

I bent down hurriedly and scrabbled on the floor, and just then I heard a muttered sentence in English, followed by something in French—or could I even make out the delicate whooshing consonants of Russian? 'She's a good European…' Was *that* what he said? Was he suggesting that

Patricia Highsmith, the American thriller writer, was a good European? Since she set many of her novels in Germany, or Italy, or France, that could have been his meaning. On the other hand, I thought, surely the real European was Nabokov himself, whose characters seemed to live in a sumptuous mid-European world of imagination, even when they were pursuing Lolita across the United States or evoking a Russian childhood.

I was never able to tell him this. I never had the chance to find out what exactly it was he said at that moment because he left the lobby soon afterwards with the very slightest of bows in our direction, off no doubt to his private apartment on the top floor of the Grand Hotel with its view over the shimmering Lac Léman.

But I do know the feeling I had—the feeling that had grown within me ever since I had come to live in Switzerland with my first husband, David—that I was feeling my way around in a sort of microcosm of the world's cultural mosaic, or at least of Europe's cultural mosaic. Switzerland was decidedly cosmopolitan. Indeed, on one level it was highly international. Many Swiss spoke reasonably fluent English. Geneva was famous for hosting the United Nations Office and many other global organizations. Tourists and skiers of every nationality flocked to the Swiss Alps. There were international music festivals in Lucerne and film festivals in Locarno. Writers, artists, and musicians from all over the world made Switzerland their home.

And yet, despite this veneer of internationalism, for all the division of Switzerland into French-speaking, Italian-speaking, and German-speaking provinces or cantons, the Swiss themselves often struck me as being remarkably provincial. And this *Provinzialismus*, as the Swiss Germans, themselves, called it, was a source of pride. They *liked* their French, German, Romansch, or Italian habits; they liked the way their own canton did things, and they liked their own take on the European national cultures that partly defined them.

When I first went to live with David in Zürich, a life that included visits to his parents in the Züri Oberland, I learned High German. Why? Because I found out that speaking English was not an easy way to become an insider with the Swiss, despite many of them speaking English as a second, third, or even fourth language. My learning High German was an attempt to get a bit more warmth and acceptance into my conversations with David's family, friends, and colleagues.

It didn't work. It took me at least two years to discover that the only possibility for really getting on with Swiss Germans was to speak Swiss German—or at least to learn enough phrases in Swiss German to be allowed into the charmed circle. My High German, which was more or less grammatically correct, got me nowhere—or at least only to the outer fringes of politeness.

However, as soon as I started using my newly minted Swiss German, the doors to friendship and acceptance were suddenly flung open. No longer was I the rather aloof English ghost at the banquet. I became instantly 'one of us'. It didn't matter if I made lots of mistakes. The effort was what counted. Somehow my stumbling Swiss German signaled I was ready to become one of them rather than remain rooted in my world of 'just like me'.

This was all way back in the 1970s and 1980s. However, I doubt much has changed with the Swiss 'cantonal' mentality since—despite the advances in global English, the 24/7 high-speed connectivity via the Internet, the cross-border mergers and acquisitions, the relocation of multinational headquarters to Switzerland. However flattened the world has become, and however many Chinese are now learning English (400 million at the last estimate), however much air travel has made global markets more accessible, the ability to understand and adapt to different local cultures—such as the Swiss German—continues to mark the difference between success and failure in the new global economy.

My time in Switzerland taught me not only to appreciate the cultural differences between French, Italian, and German parts of the country, it also showed me a form of multiculturalism in action that was completely foreign to my sheltered Anglo-Saxon upbringing.

I had grown up as a schoolboy in South London, in an England that was largely monocultural at the time. Okay, I met students from other countries at Cambridge, where I studied and lived for seven years. But despite the Commonwealth bursaries and scholarships, Cambridge was nothing like the colorful melting pot of cultures and races that it has since become. I was born and bred a white English boy from a middle-class white background. I spoke only one language, and thought only one way, and believed the whole world was more or less 'just like me'.

So imagine my surprise to fall in love with a Swiss German—through a common acquaintance at Cambridge—and be transported to a world of *Grüezi Mitenand* (Morning, everyone), *Sechsel*äuten (Spring Festival) parades in Zürich's backstreets, *Züri Geschnetzeltes mit Rösti* (Sliced Veal with Potatoes), and autumn trekking in the foothills of the Matterhorn. My cultural intelligence (CQ) journey had begun.

BECOMING A BAMBOO LEADER

We are all on a CQ journey every day of our lives in this rich, complex, and sometimes deeply unsettling world. In our businesses, families, and relationships, we connect as a matter of course with people from every culture. I am by no means different in talking regularly via Skype to clients and contacts in Australia, Brazil, the US, France, Japan, and Hong Kong, to name just a few of the countries and locations. Whether for business, family, or pleasure, I get on a plane to Denmark, Singapore, Italy, South Korea, or even Myanmar as if it were nothing special, as if the destination were just around the corner.

In this sense I am something of a mini-multinational, just like millions of entrepreneurs and small or medium-size businesses like me around the world—and millions of tourists too. Even at home in London, I interact regularly with different members of multicultural teams in companies both large and small, as well as with their corresponding teams in countries all over the globe. Almost everything I do involves some kind of cross-cultural element. I exercise three times a week at my local gym by the River Thames in a BODYPUMP class where it only recently occurred to me to count how many nationalities were in the studio.

The result astounded me. I discovered that I take regular exercise with BODYPUMPers of around thirty-five nations, of which just two 'locally grown' fitness fanatics (including myself) represent the UK. Our instructors are Brazilian, Cypriot, Hong Kong Chinese, and Latvian. And yet, until I did my little study—which eased the pain of the countless lower-half lunges—it did not occur to me that there was anything special in our thrice-weekly cultural mash-up. Or rather, it occurred to me on some level where my cultural intelligence was on automatic—the space where I translated what was said to me in different versions of English, with a few Portuguese or Greek words thrown in, and where I instinctively modulated my own Cambridge English to chime with different ways of speaking the language.

In other words, my BODYPUMP class is a microcosm of what I have trained my CQ to do over the past forty years: tune in, accept, interpret, respond with similar intonation and even choice of words, harmonize, gain trust, make friendships, gain benefits.

I don't know whether this strikes a chord with you or not. It's only a simple example, but I'm sure if you think over your daily routine in your workplace or at home, you might come up with similar examples of almost unnoticed adapting or, as some of the CQ studies call it, 'flexing'. It may be the way you talk with your local corner shop owner on the way to work, or the regulars at your coffee shop, or colleagues on your team, or your boss. It's something we do in the face of the incredible diversity of our world, both in the workplace and when communicating via virtual networks. We try to get on the other person's wavelength.

We may not be very good at it. We may have little experience of it. We may be better with understanding and adapting to some cultures rather than others. But I think, if you go deep inside, you will catch glimpses of moments when this reaching out or flexing, or whatever you want to call it, really worked for you. A moment of much deeper understanding. A moment of curiosity crowned with a flash of enlightenment. A moment of greater tolerance, or compassion, or simply human warmth. A moment when you bridged that gap with a person from another background almost without thinking—and yet retained the essential being that is you, with all your values and beliefs intact. I call a person who regularly achieves this level of understanding and flexibility a Bamboo Leader. The bamboo bends in the wind, but it is inherently very strong. It is still used for scaffolding in some parts of the world. It flexes with wind, and rain, and even snow but always springs back. It has an empty centre with space to be filled.

In other words, the bamboo presents both empathy and strength. As the world becomes more multipolar, more connected, and more multicultural, we need to develop the qualities of the Bamboo Leader in ourselves. That is the journey I'd like to guide you on in this book—a journey to becoming more Bamboo Strong in today's global economy.

DO YOU SPEAK SWISS GERMAN ?

When I talk about a 'cultural intelligence journey', I don't mean that we are all more or less passengers bound in the same direction as soon as we consciously step on the CQ Express—and that we're all going to end up at the same destination once we have crossed similar mountains, and rivers, and national borders, and cultural barriers.

We all respond differently to the challenges of this complex, cross-cultural world of ours, and each one of us is different and individual. We will have personal and individual reactions to different cultural settings and scenarios. It is by no means certain where we will end up even when we have developed our cultural intelligence over many years and in many different situations. Your CQ Express might take you anywhere.

For some people—and these tend to be the majority—it is extremely difficult to function successfully when confronted with cultures and attitudes that are not very similar to their own. Even when they are posted to other countries in their jobs, they often fail to adapt to the prevailing culture or to even set foot outside their own safe expatriate ghetto. They want everyone they encounter to be 'just like me' and to do things 'just like at home'. And when that doesn't work out for them, they complain to their expatriate colleagues that they don't 'get' the Chinese, or the Brazilians, or the Indians.

They want a system that will enable them to interact safely with the locals, or people from the same region, without having to make any adjustments in their values or behaviour. Lists of dos and don'ts are often the main support that such professionals use (if they use any), as if a quick rundown of etiquette tips will save them the painful business of overcoming cultural differences and communicating effectively.

This shopping list approach to cultural adjustment is perhaps better than making no effort at all. However, it is unlikely to work when you are confronted (as we all are, sometimes several times a day) by a multiplicity of different cultural situations—ethnic, generational, or organizational. How do you handle the East Asia portfolio of clients you have been handed when you are told the Japanese are different to the South Koreans, who are different to the Mainland Chinese, who are different to the Taiwanese? How do you avoid stereotypes when you rely on your etiquette tips and shopping lists? How do you treat a Japanese-American differently to a Tokyo-born Japanese?

Don't get me wrong. A list is an attempt at understanding or fitting in, but it won't help you respond effectively to a variety of cultural contexts. You will become confused when trying to remember what to do when and in what culture. You will get cultural overload, and you will do what many stressed people do: say it's all a waste of time, stick to your guns, and not bother.

This is a great shame because with a little help to flex your cultural muscles, you could end up like I have in my BODYPUMP class. You could instinctively adjust to different peoples from different cultures almost without noticing you are doing it. After the class is over, I spend some time exchanging a few words in Italian with Fabrizio, the barista at the club's coffee bar. Fabrizio clearly enjoys these little chats and often offers me a salmon and salad panino on the house to accompany my double macchiato. It is not a premeditated ruse on my part. I don't have a list to tell me that Italians like hand gestures and exaggerated flattery. I just do what comes naturally. I try a little cultural intelligence and *voilà!* (Or rather, *ecco!)*

You might say that all this proves is that we should treat people as individuals. And you would be right. Beyond the cultural differences, we often find that people are the same all over the world. They have the same needs, and insecurities, and loves, and dreams that we have.

However, to discover and celebrate this, you have to make some effort to get on the same wavelength, to reach out and communicate, and above all to respect others' beliefs and traditions. Cultural intelligence, which also includes cultural sensitivity, helps you to do this.

In Switzerland, I discovered that speaking English did not make me a trusted member of my Swiss family, not even High German did. I had to speak Swiss German and *make the effort* to become accepted. If you take the example of Switzerland out into today's global economy, you will find that English being spoken almost everywhere does not mean that we are all more less the same and on the same wavelength. There are many local versions of English, all with their own dialect and expressions and meanings. English is also a second or perhaps a third language in vast areas of the planet. Your English is not necessarily my English. You are not me. Yes, we are living in an era of extraordinary innovation, convergence, and connectivity. However, the great paradox is that the more we are connected, and the smaller the world seems, the more we have to respond effectively to new markets and cultures that were previously hidden from us. We are virtually present now and sometimes physically present in Shanghai and Bangalore, in Yangon, and Sao Paolo. How do we grasp the opportunities? How do we communicate? How do we show the necessary respect and not come over as Neanderthals with an excess of arrogance?

If you want to succeed as a Bamboo Leader, you will have to speak the equivalent of some Swiss German in a world of English. You will have to relate, to listen, and to adapt, and only then will you develop the skills to successfully lead.

GLOBAL AGILITY

Let's talk about those skills.

Or rather, let's start off by talking about what an absence of those skills looks like.

In the 1990s, I worked for a major international bank in Hong Kong. This bank has deep roots in China and operations all over Asia, and indeed all over the world. You would think that such a bank, with its advertising slogan that mentioned the words 'local' and 'global', would have high standards of cultural intelligence. It would need not only to understand its customers in many countries, but it would also need to motivate, manage, and inspire its highly multicultural workforce. However, the bank had a colonial legacy to deal with, which meant that even in the late 1990s the senior management in Hong Kong was almost entirely made up of Caucasians or, to put it more precisely, white British males.

It wasn't until the return of Hong Kong to Chinese sovereignty in 1997 that an ethnic Chinese was promoted to the role of general manager. So for a long time in the build-up to the handover, the bank was promoting its deep local roots and Chinese background without a single Chinese in a senior position. The bank defended this by saying that it had a meritocratic human resources system that promoted only on merit and not on quotas.

Fair enough, you might think. But if the result was to look hypocritical and out of touch at the most significant moment in the bank's history, you might wonder why no ethnic Chinese had been sufficiently developed to merit inclusion in the senior ranks. In addition, due to the example at the top, I encountered daily incidents of what might be called 'looking down on the Chinese' from those who should have known better. The bank has since developed a world-leading diversity and inclusion programme, which has seen a Chinese woman installed as CEO in Hong Kong and many other ethnic Chinese in senior executive positions. I am sure the air of superiority of one ethnic group, occasional and fitful as it was, has long since disappeared. However, my experience suggests that low CQ can easily damage a corporate culture as well as the bottom line. It was perhaps no accident that the bank's profitability increased when it became less visibly 'colonial' and far more 'Chinese' following the handover.

Low CQ means that you don't ask questions about new cultural situations; you don't think deeply about what might be going wrong, and you don't adjust accordingly. High CQ allows you to be agile in different cultural settings or in response to new cultural challenges, whether these come from a multicultural workforce with diverse religious beliefs, a company's expansion into new markets, disruptive innovations and technologies, or perhaps from a conference hall full of people from many different backgrounds.

Responsiveness and sensitivity are what count—and you can't build this high CQ in one day. However, you can learn from the mistakes around you to develop your cultural intelligence skills over time. Research suggests that exposure to a variety of cultural experiences in different countries, and an ability to adapt *even when making mistakes*, develops a much higher level of CQ than living and working in one particular overseas location.

Those who are asked to react and solve problems in new cultural settings become, almost literally, 'wired'. And this can be true even when they fail in their first or second or third posting or relocation. Perhaps especially when they fail.

It seems that those with heightened CQ are able to pick themselves up and dust themselves off every time they fall flat on their face. And this resilience, or what I call Bamboo

Strong, has enormous implications for business leaders, NGOS and charitable organizations, government agencies, universities, even military planners and strategists, in the multicultural future that is already upon us.

Low CQ may partially explain why Western countries and governments have so signally failed in planning for the future of countries in which they have intervened, such as Iraq and Afghanistan. As Rory Stewart, the British adventurer and diplomat, explains in his book, *The Prince of the Marshes* (about his time as an administrator in Southern Iraq), ignorance of centuries of tribalism, local cultures, rivalries, and loyalties, has led to many of the mistakes that Western governments have made in the Middle East and Central Europe in recent times. The same mistakes have been replicated time and again by companies or organizations expanding into culturally diverse markets they haven't understood, or which they believe are part of the new 'global village' and therefore easily susceptible to their global brand and management style.

Google is just one of many large foreign companies that has failed in China because they made elementary cultural mistakes, such as choosing the Chinese characters for *Gu* and *Ge* as their name brand because they sounded like Google.

The characters translated into Chinese as 'Song of the Rice Harvest'. Chinese consumers were not especially enthused to be considered aspiring rice farmers.

These failures of research and targeting—and especially the inability to understand or reach out to local cultures— are extremely costly. Many international charities, businesses, and government programs are not only ineffective but lose millions or even billions of dollars. And yet, if you told some CEOs or business leaders that low cultural intelligence was severely impacting their profitability, they might think you were cuckoo. The same might be said of politicians or military leaders who think that CQ is of little importance in the overarching priorities of a political campaign or military intervention.

The very word 'culture' suggests concerts and paintings, poetry and novels. Together with 'intelligence', it might indicate something to do with universities or bookishness in general. For many business people intent on profitable expansion, cultural intelligence sounds like a luxury, something rather soft and fluffy, a minor branch of human resources—or at the most a series of tips on etiquette and behaviour.

And yet leaders who are Bamboo Strong know that CQ is hard core. They know that their success depends on it.

NO BRAINERS FOR PERFORMANCE

I will let you in on a secret.

The reason I can speak authoritatively about the failure that derives from low cultural intelligence is because I've been there.

Before I arrived in Hong Kong in the late 1980s, I spent a year living and working in Japan. This was my first experience of a Far Eastern country, and I felt naturally drawn to it by all I had seen in Japanese movies and read in Japanese novels. I knew it was aesthetically beautiful in parts, had a long cultural history, was a center for Buddhism in the East, and was imbued with a powerful work ethic.

To be frank, I thought I could fall in love there too. I had separated from David after a decade together, and I was hopeful that somehow in romantic Japan I would meet someone—a Japanese or a *gaijin* (literally 'outside person')—who would bowl me off my feet. How wrong I was. It wasn't necessarily Japan's fault—after all, I prepared myself well by learning some basic Japanese and, using my cultural intelligence radar, choosing to rent a typical small Japanese apartment with a four-square tatami lounge, little kitchen, and balcony in a delightful little suburb of Tokyo called Nishi-Koyama. The main street was hung with tinkling mobile cherry blossoms. I remember that sound accompanying me home from the subway station every day as I walked past bookstores, and pharmacies, and mini-supermarkets, and pachinko parlors. It was all very local, and almost no other foreigners lived there.

You would think this was the perfect set-up for entering Japanese life and making Japanese friends. Wrong again. If anything, my hesitant Japanese alienated local people—or rather, it did nothing to change their permanently polite, completely unreadable attitude towards me. I exchanged politeness ten times a day and made absolutely no social headway. I was, in a word, a *gaijin*.

Even when my Japanese improved, and I made an extensive tour of the country by local trains to collect material for a book, I always had the feeling that I remained on the outside of Japanese life. To some extent this may have been due to Japanese suspicion of the foreigner—the xenophobia that some of my *gaijin* friends claimed was rife in Japanese society—but the curious thing was I never felt hostility. I simply felt a rather lowly person on the social ladder, someone who deserved ritual politeness and a pleasant smile in a bar but who was destined to be on the outside looking in.

Nevertheless, my basic cultural knowledge and especially my handy Japanese phrases (English was not spoken much, even in Tokyo) got me to train stations and into taxis and hotels—except for the Japanese-style inns on weekends, which were usually reserved for Japanese guests.

Perhaps if I had hung out more in places like Roppongi, which was an expatriate enclave in the city, I would have made more contacts and friends, at least among other *gaijin*. But I was stubborn. I didn't want to admit defeat. I didn't want to be yet another cog in the expatriate world, mixing only with other expatriates and speaking English all the time. In short, I wanted to continue exploring, even if it meant failing.

Deep down I may also have known that I was learning. I saw parts of Japan that perhaps few other foreigners had seen, simply by going way off the beaten track in my train journeys to the northernmost tip of Honshu or the inner mountains of Shikoku. I did form some very basic, if transitory, friendships with some local Japanese I met on my travels, who helped me in my researches into Japanese business and daily life.

It was as if I were trying to build up my vocabulary of cultural intelligence. I was flexing regardless, learning how to communicate through instinct and body language as much as through language. These skills greatly helped me in my later relationships with business teams, clients, and counterparts, not only in Asia but also throughout the world. Almost everyone who has worked across cultures has faced a similar feeling of isolation, of being left out or being completely out of step. It's natural in the process of learning, and in many ways it's essential to the process of learning.

This doesn't have to take place in a foreign land. You might feel confused as part of the leadership team in your home base—perhaps in North America, UK, Europe, or Australasia—when your company acquires operations in China or Brazil, Poland or India. Suddenly, you have to handle new ways of doing business, running meetings, negotiating contracts, or making decisions that are markedly different to your usual ways of functioning. You have to relate to and inspire work teams from several different cultures.

How do you respond? Do you go out there and try to figure out what the differences are? Do you carry on as normal and expect the Chinese, European, Indian, or Latin American businesses to fall into line? Do you replace the local CEOs with people from your home team? Or do you bring Chinese, Brazilian, Polish, or Indian executives onto your headquarters team?

There are many ways to respond, but one thing is sure: *you have to respond.* You have to discover how to work successfully across cultures. And you can only do this if you and your team have developed some level of CQ, preferably through experience (and probably mistakes or failure) in overseas markets, or through specific CQ coaching and mentoring, or a mixture of both.

Business dislikes ambiguity.

And yet uncertainty or ambiguity is exactly what many companies, entrepreneurs, and organizations face in this increasingly complex world of new frontiers, mass migration, and cultural diversity. Companies want their leaders to deal with ambiguity. New cross-cultural challenges present themselves every day in the form of an inexplicably hostile email, in the puzzled or unresponsive audience at a presentation, in a misfiring local community campaign. In almost every sphere of our life and performance—including the commitment of many people to making the world a better place through charitable activities, or environmental and human rights platforms—we are required to think and respond with cultural intelligence.

CQ is a no brainer to inspire performance, and so is the likelihood of failure. If you don't fail somewhere along the line, you cannot develop the higher level of CQ that this constant flow of intercultural challenges sends your way. The benefits in terms of performance often become evident over time. When I moved on from Japan to work in the corporate world in Hong Kong, I found that cultural intelligence affected my decision-making and my ability to manage risk. Quite simply, it helped me make informed decisions rather than impulsive ones.

In the same way, CQ can help you negotiate successfully across cultures or interpret your counterparts' silences. In many ambiguous situations, it gives you nonverbal clues and strategies for creating commonly understood goals with parties from a different culture.

THE KARAOKE TEST
('DON'T CRY FOR ME ARGENTINA')

I have a Czech friend in London who works for a major bank, which recently sent him to Melbourne with a one-day stopover in Singapore for client meetings. The stopover was followed by a non-stop flight to Melbourne, where he spent half a day at meetings before flying back to London via Dubai the same evening. I think he spent something like forty-eight hours or more in the air and managed three or four business meetings.

He was stressed. He's only about twenty-eight, and yet every time I meet him at the gym he's stressed, usually from flying somewhere or other and dealing with different cultures and people of different backgrounds. They're part of his portfolio. They're his responsibility.

However, what impresses me always about Jan is his buoyancy. The stress of business travel and strange hotels never seems to get him down. He's always smiling and laughing, even after forty-eight hours in the air! And I think I know why. He's married to Gracia, an Indonesian, and whenever they have free time they travel (again) to his family in the Czech Republic or her family in the Philippines, or to one of their favorite Asian countries like Malaysia. He's always talking about the Asian foods he adores, or how he and Gracia miss their adventures in Denpasar or Chiang Mai or Shanghai. In other words, he's a cross-cultural global citizen with high CQ.

Jan and Gracia don't mind discomfort at all, whether it's physical or emotional. They don't mind being jolted out of their usual mindset and way of doing things. In fact, they welcome cross-cultural challenges. I don't think Jan knows every single aspect of etiquette when he goes to those many different countries he has to visit. He often tells me about his latest faux-pas: how he walked into a meeting in Shanghai ahead of the most senior person in the Chinese party or tried to shake hands with his Muslim mother-in-law when he met her for the first time.

Business travellers like Jan, who take pleasure from exercising their cultural intelligence, are much less likely to suffer from burnout and mental exhaustion than those who remain fiercely protected and closed off in their familiar world: Western-style hotel, business district, 'international' restaurants and bars. The same applies to expatriate managers who spend all their time in their sanitized office space, residential areas 'for foreigners', and Western-style entertainment districts where the clubs are filled with many more expatriates than locals.

In my experience in the international bank in Hong Kong, the really successful and fulfilled expatriates were the ones who respected the Chinese and others from different ethnic backgrounds, worked collaboratively with them, maybe spoke some phrases of Cantonese, and made some effort to socialize or even participate in family gatherings, birthdays, or festivals with the local Chinese on their team. They always seemed to be far happier than the expatriates— and there were a considerable number of them—who stuck to their own kind, their own ways, and rarely mingled. I call it my Karaoke Test. If I could imagine going out after dinner with a group of local professionals and joining in with them at a karaoke bar, or even in one of those air-conditioned box rooms that were equipped with microphones and A/V systems and food and drink menus in Hong Kong, I knew I could succeed. You don't have to get hopelessly drunk, although it sometimes seemed that some Chinese, Japanese, or Korean groups specialized in this, but you have to be willing to sing at least one, preferably two or three, songs, *and obviously enjoy it*, to be accepted. If you can hum along with a local song, and even attempt a few phrases in

Chinese, or Japanese, or Korean from reading and singing the subtitles, so much the better. Then you are a *real* local!

I never quite understood the passion with which my hosts or clients or professional colleagues embraced these beer- or sake-fuelled evenings after dinner (or sometimes during dinner in China). But I sure as hell did it. After a few outings, I became reasonably proficient in 'Don't Cry For Me Argentina' or 'New York, New York', or 'My Way', and could belt it out with the best of them.

I lost count of the number of good business deals or relationships that came about because of those evenings.

Of course, business leaders and CEOs might have to find more elegant ways to socialize with their local clients and customers than singing karaoke—although in China and Japan the practice seems to go almost to the top, even in local government and government circles. However, what I call the Karaoke Test remains the same for all cultures. If you can socialize successfully, show respect, and enjoy local traditions and customs, you will be far happier and have greater job satisfaction than people of lower CQ who cut themselves off or fail to enjoy the challenge.

THE PROFIT MOTIVE

However, it's not all about job satisfaction. CQ improves the bottom line too.

Companies and organizations that incorporate CQ into their business and organizational culture are far more likely to be profitable—and make less costly mistakes—than those that don't.

CQ strategies often go hand in hand with enlightened and energetic diversity and inclusion programs. Global multinationals such as BP, Shell, Apple, General Motors, Ford, Standard Chartered, and Barclays have strong CQ as well as diversity and inclusion policies. Studies undertaken by the Cultural Intelligence Center have shown that the vast majority of companies that include cultural intelligence in their training, hiring, and strategizing show a marked increase in profits, not counting the costs saved from the kind of cultural mistakes and poorly targeted marketing that damaged companies like Tesco and Walmart in China.

The research indicates that leaders who are Bamboo Strong see the benefits of hiring, promoting, and rewarding people with high CQ. Through their cross-cultural skills in negotiating and networking, such people generate increased opportunities and profits for their organizations, both saving and earning money. As a result, they are often in demand and are likely to earn more than their less culturally flexible peers.

An organisation that spans many cultures, both internationally and in their home market, will benefit from executives who can move easily between different cultures and ways of thinking. Those individuals who can adapt their own and the company's global mindset to local cultures, and respond effectively to the inevitable misunderstandings and clashes that arise daily in cross-cultural encounters, are increasingly in demand.

Say you were asked to choose someone for your team who could move with relative ease between the cultures and markets of Latin America, Africa, India, and China. Would you choose the person with proven cultural intelligence, the one who had already earned you money in some of those markets and built relationships and networks, or would you choose someone who had a record of conflict, stubbornness, arrogance, or misunderstanding when dealing with different markets?

FINDING UTOPIA—OR EVERYWHERE

I should add a word of caution here.

Simply being internationally minded or aware of the differences between Italian and German culture, or Mexican and Chinese, or Japanese and Korean, does not mean that you will inevitably operate successfully within these cultures or between them. Some organizations, such as the bank I worked for in Hong Kong, have international cadres who undertake short-term training for different parts of the world and are always ready to be posted elsewhere.

However, in my experience such international cadres are not especially proficient in cultural intelligence. They bring with them the air that they are only working in that particular country because they have been sent there. Although they may have some basic knowledge about, say, South Korea or the United Arab Emirates, they radiate a certain superiority of belonging to the central, English-speaking leadership team in the bank's home headquarters. Not all are like this, but a surprising number are.

In the new global economy it is much more difficult to impose the attitudes and working styles of the Western 'boss class' on colleagues from the developing markets. Western companies have discovered that it makes much more economic sense to have a local boss running operations in those markets rather than imposing someone from outside the culture. Indeed, the Western part of the company's business may now be subsidiary to the multinational's operations in Asia Pacific, China, India, the Middle East, or Latin America. Western expatriates are often working under a non-Western CEO.

It is therefore essential to have local teams and leaders from these cultures, and for Western teams to learn how to communicate and work together with them in order to generate greater profits all round. Investment is flowing into Australia and New Zealand, the UK and Northern Europe, the US and Canada from many Asian countries, including India and China. The momentum of mergers and acquisitions is moving from the West to the East. I read recently that China's venture capitalists are acquiring majority stakes in American and British dating websites. There is no reversing or changing the direction of these newly invigorating flows.

Cultural intelligence will be required more and more as the world's economies become more connected. In 1516, the English philosopher and statesman Sir Thomas More published a book called *Utopia* ('Nowhere'), in which he imagined a complex, self-contained world set on an island where fifty-four diverse communities shared a common culture and way of life.

The citizens of Utopia shared their surpluses with one another, helped one another out, and built a store of gold to be prepared for any disaster. They were wealthy, but they didn't display their wealth. They despised lavish clothes and ostentatious displays of power as being divisive and vulgar. So the ambassadors from nearby countries dressed modestly when they visited them and behaved according to the Utopians' ascetic customs. Hence these neighbors became friends and allies of the Utopians, and they traded successfully with each other to benefit the region.

One day, however, ambassadors from the more distant country of Anemolia arrived in Utopia dressed resplendently in gold and finery and acting like gods with an attitude problem. The result was that they clashed violently with the Utopians, who drove them out of their kingdom.

This clash of cultures would have been avoidable if the Anemolians had shown more cultural intelligence. Nowadays we live in a globalized world where Utopia is not an imagined Nowhere. It is a very real and accessible Everywhere. This world is all around us at the touch of a keyboard. Every island, every country, and every culture is open to us if we just know how to make allies and friends. CQ offers us a means to work effectively within this world, to navigate the waters of misunderstanding and the rapids of potential conflict.

Ultimately, CQ is not just about ostentatious wealth, power, or even individual well-being and success. It is about creating a better world, in which local rivalries, the clash of religions and cultures, the fanaticism we hear about daily on the news are connected to a bigger picture of tolerance and mutual understanding. Without reaching out and trying to understand other cultures and ways of doing things, we are condemned to parochialism, missed opportunities, and unnecessary rancor. Cultural intelligence is hard work. But it's definitely worth it.

To create your own Cultural Intelligence (CQ) Planner, with action points and strategies from this chapter, please visit www.davidcliveprice.com/planner

COURAGE

CQ Drive

PEOPLE LIKE US

Now we've talked about what cultural intelligence is, we can talk about the courage that's needed to implement it.

You will find that not everyone has the inner motivation or the determination to set out on the CQ journey. Many give up, even before they reach the first steps of training to acquire new cultural knowledge. They don't see the point. They think it's too difficult. They give it low priority amidst all the business of being posted abroad with their families or of taking on a new responsibility at home.

They may pay lip service to it and go along to a cultural training or two, because they're told they should. However, as soon as they're faced with a real challenge, they give up and retreat back to their tried and tested expatriate circle or let other people do the intercultural 'hard yards'. They remain marooned on an island of People Like Us.

Finding the necessary courage and confidence to take on the challenges and conflicts of cross-cultural situations is not always easy. And it's not for everyone. However, the good news is that CQ courage can be developed. Let me begin by telling you about one of the biggest cultural challenges in my own life.

It's about a novel I wanted to write.

In the late 1970s I was living a blissful and peaceful existence in the Italian countryside near Siena. I had moved from Cambridge, where I had completed my Ph.D., to my life in Switzerland with David, and then to the University of Bologna on a British Academy fellowship to complete my post-doctoral studies on musical patrons in the Italian Renaissance. It was in the midst of all this esoteric research—and learning Italian and going deeper into my passion for Italian culture—that I decided I didn't want to be an academic after all. I wanted to see the world and write books: travel and business books, novels, translations of Italian literature, anything but academic history.

So I hit on the idea of renting a mill in some forgotten corner of Tuscany—near an Etruscan hilltop town called Volterra—and of combining writing my first book with open-air life and learning better Italian. David was also keen on the idea, so after a few months in the rented mill, we decided to buy a farmhouse together in the same valley as the mill for an amazingly cheap price, even in those days. David came down from his work in Switzerland on alternate weekends, and meanwhile I started to write. I also started to cultivate the abandoned olives, and vines, and vegetable plots that lined the terraces from the farmhouse down into the stream at the bottom of the valley. After all that academic work, I took to Italian farm life with a passion that was greatly encouraged by my friendships with the local farmers. They taught me how to prune olives and vines, create vegetable plots, and harvest the fruits of my labors. My Italian came on in leaps and bounds.

The problem was the novel. You can't control inspiration. It comes and finds you whether you like it or not, often with ideas that seem quite outlandish.

My first book, *The Other Italy*, was all about my valley, and the farmers, and the peaceful beauties of the rural Italy I encountered. However, the idea for my second book was almost diametrically opposite.

Sometime during all that pruning of vines, and digging around the olive trees, and cutting down bamboo to use for tomato canes, and snipping cypress fronds to bind the grapes, I got an idea for a novel about a gay man finding his identity. He would come out to his family, colleagues, friends in a way that was both exhilarating and liberating.

Of course, to some extent the narrator was going to be me because I had been through that painful experience with my own family and my circle at Cambridge. But the idea for the novel suggested to me a setting that was far more dramatic than that of closeted gay academic goes to Switzerland and makes a new life.

At that time, New York and San Francisco were the hubs of gay sub-culture, much more so than placid and still very conservative England. As I had heard from David and others who had visited the States, these cities were also melting pots of cultures and peoples from all over the globe. If I wanted to write a novel about an academic gay man liberating himself from the weight of a deceitful marriage and a conventional past, I had to set it in New York—and perhaps also in the form of a journey across the States. Above all, if I wanted my hero to be shaken from his certainties, I should make him encounter not only sexual difference but also racial and ethnic differences.

I don't know exactly why I wanted all this in my valley of sylvan bliss in northern Italy, but there it was. I couldn't possibly write such a novel without going to New York or across the States to the West Coast. Having spent seven years in Cambridge, and with a few years' experience of Swiss bourgeois life, an Italian university, and an abandoned farm, I knew little or nothing about big cities—and I had never been to America.

So I was faced with this rather terrifying choice: either go to New York and give up a comfortable existence for now, or don't write the novel. Let it literally wither on the vine, as it would do after a few months. I told myself it wouldn't make any money. I would jeopardize this idyllic life I had created, I had no experience as a novelist, I had no skin in the game.

And then one afternoon, I found myself researching gay bars and the Lower East Village in Manhattan. I discovered that the area to the east and south of the Lower East Side was made up of avenues called Avenues A, B, C, etc. I saw there was a famous gay bar on Second Avenue nearby. I had the title of my novel—*Alphabet City*!

Why did I have the courage to come up with this idea?

And most of all, how did I turn this initial glimmer of courage into what became a successful novel?

Perhaps all that moving between cultures after I left my Cambridge ivory tower had prepared me for it. I knew I had a passion for Italy—after all, I had studied the Renaissance at university—and my biggest dream was to learn Italian and more about Italian culture. I didn't realize then that I would do more than study Italian culture: I would live an Italian life. I didn't know that I would have a Swiss husband ('friend' was the term used then) after I came out, or that I would learn basic Swiss German. I didn't know that I would start speaking Italian with a Tuscan soft *c* as in *hoca-hola* and become an *inglese italianizzato*.

But I guess that every new learning experience was preparing me for New York. And it didn't stop there. Because I already knew some of the benefits of cultural intelligence, I overcame my fear of visiting gay bars in Second Avenue, of renting a cheap apartment in the most dangerous area of the

Lower East Side, and of taking a Greyhound bus trip from Phoenix, Arizona, to Los Angeles.

In other words, overcoming my fears took me beyond People Like Us to fresh visions of the world.

ONLY CONNECT

Now I am not suggesting that everyone who wants to develop their CQ must go out and have strange new experiences, or travel to odd or dangerous locations, or put themselves in survive-or-die situations.

It may be that at some time in your life you are placed in a challenging cross-cultural environment, or it may be that your challenges come in a more measured way through work situations, relocations for your business, or independent travel to one of the many newly accessible destinations of the world. Almost every day of our lives we are faced with cross-cultural encounters through the Internet and digital connectivity, or simply through meeting people of different cultural backgrounds. The point is that we are being asked to connect—and one of the starting places for our connecting is the imagination. If I hadn't imagined what it might be like in New York City in comparison to the life I had in Italy, I might not have summoned enough courage to go there. If I had relied on my stereotypes of what New Yorkers were like ('loud, argumentative, and liable to tell people to go f-themselves'), I might not have made the New Yorker friends I did of every race and background. I might not have had the added benefit of my fictional hero falling in love with an African-American painter.

All my stereotypes were blown apart by the New York I experienced and wrote about. To some extent I connected because I was gay. That very personal interest helped me relate to the multiracial subculture of the East Village. But there were other interests too: poetry, painting, classical music, writing, and Italian, Asian, and Jewish food. Indeed, *Alphabet City* takes as one of its themes Otherness, and the mysterious attraction of gaining access to people and worlds we don't know.

If we use our imaginations and our passions, there is almost no culture or people that we cannot discover through one or other of our interests, or through a rich combination of these interests. It may be sport, it may be business, it may be fashion or photography, it may be language. As E.M. Forster, the novelist and forensic observer of the Anglo-Indian experience, wrote as an epigraph to *Howard's End*, 'Only connect'.

Today we are asked to connect more and more, but we often hold ourselves back though a lack of courage, or imagination, or both. When faced with mass migrations in Europe, or demagoguery against a certain country or followers of a religion, or the simplistic association of Islam with terror organisations, or any of the other great issues of our times that require cross-cultural nuance and understanding, it is easy to fall back on fear, stereotyping, and a lack of imaginative courage.

The key to all these cross-cultural endeavors is to connect. And for this, our passions and interests—as well as our previous experiences of flexing—are great motivators and bridges.

RIDING ON FEAR

I've often told myself that I'm afraid of something in another culture. Haven't you?

I was absurdly afraid to join in the *ballo liscio* (pure dance) at my local Italian bar, where the farmers and their wives danced their traditional country polkas with such confidence and elegance. I was afraid of walking home from Second Avenue back to my apartment on the Lower East Side. I was always looking behind me.

There is an odd reverse psychology in this—the fear that seems to almost paralyze you, but you do it anyway. It suggests that in cross-cultural encounters you can use the power of fear to your own advantage. For example, I learned that the best way to dance in the *ballo liscio* was simply to let myself go and be the follower. The result was I became an admired participant in a whole network of farmer exchanges in the valley: fresh produce at my front door, borrowed tractors, free transport to the olive cooperative, and a thousand other benefits. I forced myself to walk home every night from that Second Avenue bar in New York with a casual air, not too slow and not too fast (and never drunk), to avoid a knife in the ribs from the drug pushers. What was my reward? I could wake up alert to another day of observing the fascinating characters of the Lower East Side—and put them in my novel.

It works in business situations too. When I gave a presentation to a gathering of mainly Sinhalese CEOs and business leaders in Sri Lanka during the civil war there, I inserted a passage about cultural intelligence and tolerance and mentioned the Tamils. It was a tactful reference, and it worked. Indeed, I was thanked for my awareness and sensitivity afterwards. Foolhardy perhaps, but I couldn't really stand there and say nothing about the war-torn reality outside.

The big question with fear as a motivator is this: what happens if you don't show your cultural intelligence? If I had just delivered my standard presentation for a Western audience, I would have come over as ignorant and blinkered or—worse still—as a 'superior' type who thought the world revolved around only the developed economies.

I've often used my fear of not knowing an audience or a coaching group to motivate me towards being more culturally intelligent. I always include rich local references in my speeches and keynotes for different audiences in say, Denmark, Ireland, China, or South Korea, because I know the audience will only warm to me if I show awareness of their real lives.

I learned from my time at the international bank in Hong Kong that a lack of knowledge of certain cultures could lead to significant loss of income, or even the complete failure of a venture or a new acquisition in certain parts of the world such as a new product launch in Mexico or Japan. I often wrote global speeches for the CEO and Chairman of the bank that had to be tailored specifically for the country where they were speaking. Not only did I include local references, but I also showed a historical awareness and knowledge of culture or beliefs. In other words, I sometimes had to write a dozen versions of the same speech for different countries.

Not all the bank's leaders were so sensitive. Cultural mistakes on the part of country managers often led to considerable resources being spent on clearing up the damage. Such executives were considered to be liabilities to the bank's performance. Since I didn't want to be one of those liabilities, I used my fear of cross-cultural failure to motivate me to do a good job.

I researched countries, backgrounds, traditions, and religious beliefs for my CEO's speeches. If I was unsure of the right tone and references, I talked to people within the bank from the relevant country or culture. I included a minimum of one local phrase or saying in each speech. I tried to reference at least one local festival or celebration. In short, my fear of failure or making damaging faux-pas ensured that I did my cross-cultural homework.

So the next time you find yourself hiding in a hotel lounge in a foreign country, or sticking with your group because everyone speaks English, or passing up the opportunity to go to a local restaurant with some locals in preference for the safe and 'international', remember that it's all fear deep down. And as is the way with fear, it can either hold you back— from new experiences and professional opportunities—or it can become a powerful ally to get you out into the real world.

IT'S ALL IN THE IMAGINATION

It's my belief that cultural intelligence is like a limb of the mind. The more you exercise it, the stronger it becomes.

Overcoming fear or being motivated by fear is part of the mind's training in strength and flexibility. And so too is the imagination.

I first travelled in Myanmar (Burma) in the early 1990s just after the military crackdown on the democratic winners of the 1989 elections and the imprisonment of Aung San Suu Kyi, leader of the National League of Democracy Party that had won the election. Because most Western journalists were banned following the elections, I had used the convenient fiction of travel writer to get into the country and was fortunate to have a letter signed by the ministry of tourism allowing me to travel to designated tourism spots.

I immediately found myself drawn to the northern Burmese city of Mandalay. The name had always intrigued me because of its appearance in a famous Rudyard Kipling poem:

> *By the old Moulmein Pagoda, lookin' lazy at the sea,*
> *There's a Burma girl a-settin', and I know she thinks o' me;*
> *For the wind is in the palm-trees, and the temple-bells they say:*
> *'Come you back, you British soldier; come you back to Mandalay!'*

The city also attracted me because I knew from my reading that it was the last home of King Mindon, the penultimate king of Burma before the British annexed the entire country in the late nineteenth century.

So in the winter of 1992, I took a long train journey to Mandalay from Yangon, having decided it was the best and cheapest way of seeing the country. After an uncomfortable night spent in the company of several Buddhist monks, who took great pleasure in showing me the temples and dusty towns along the railway track, and who spent most of the journey spitting out little gobbets of betel nut juice onto the carriage floor, I alighted into the chaos of Mandalay station. I had no one to greet me. I knew no one in Mandalay. The only knowledge I had of the city was what I had gleaned from books.

However, I did have one other guide to assist me on my way: my imagination. Although the streets outside the colonial arches of Mandalay railway station were illuminated only be fairy lights draped over little bars and restaurants, I set out armed with something I had envisioned in my mind as being the gateway to Mandalay: a chance encounter beneath Kipling's palm trees and the tinkling temple bells. In fact, not only did I envision a chance encounter but also I imagined meeting a local person who would like me, who would *adopt* me as a rare and exotic foreigner (an Englishman from what the Burmese call 'the big-nosed tribe'!) and introduce me to the life of the city.

And that is exactly what happened. On my way past the pagodas and the juice stands, past the curious onlookers who shuffled by in the velvet dark saying 'How are you, sir?' or 'Bicycle two dollars, sir', I bumped into the rotund figure and smiling face of Edwyn. He was wheeling a tricycle with a younger man in the passenger seat, and he immediately offered me a ride. When I told him I didn't know where I was going—perhaps to a hotel—he suggested he take me to meet his wife and their family of friends, students, and colleagues who were running a show for tourists nearby called 'Mandalay Puppets'.

Ignoring the instinctive fear in my stomach—or perhaps riding on it—I said yes. After twenty minutes cycling through streets lit only by the mosaic of chill stars overhead, I found myself sitting in an ornate puppet theatre created out of sequined tapestries and bamboo struts, being gazed down on by puppet kings, and ministers, and devils, and courtesans, all brilliantly painted in golds and reds. Edwyn and his wife, Ma Ma Naing, also ran an English school in a small area behind the stage, which meant that many of the students and theatre workers I encountered spoke some English. Within a few days, I had forged a hundred new friendships in Mandalay simply by chatting in my funny patois of simplified English mixed with a few phrases in Burmese to smooth the wheels of communication.

Friends and guides, drivers, and musicians—the whole 'tribe' associated with Mandalay Puppets—took me all over Upper Burma. They showed me how to evade military checkpoints on the way to distant places like Mogok, the ruby mining district close to the Shan State, which I almost certainly shouldn't have visited as a foreigner. I cycled with the students out to their families' farms and villages in the Mandalay hills, even though foreigners were strictly forbidden to move independently outside the city. My friends found traditional Burmese garb for me: a colored *longyi* (the Burmese sarong) that made cycling a very interesting experience, a Mandarin shirt and grey short jacket, even a Burmese cap, so that I could merge in with the population. At times I regretted the risks they took on my behalf, but my friends never complained.

It was as if I imagined how the trip would go, and then somehow it happened just like that.

I often find myself using this technique in situations that call for heightened CQ. Instead of resisting or making demands in English, instead of stating what I want out of the trip, I imagine the situation turning out as I want, and then I try to get myself *adopted*.

If you imagine yourself living in other people's worlds, you may well end up being taken under their wing. I have lived with a Chinese family in a one-roomed apartment in Hong Kong. I have spent fascinating days in a house on stilts near the banks of the River Irrawaddy in Pagan, Burma. I have lived in a farmhouse in the Cholla province of South Korea surrounded by rice fields, with garlands of dried red peppers dangling over my bed and a cow poking its head through the sliding windows. All of these experiences were of scenes formed more or less in my imagination, and they became reality due to my readiness to be helped, however briefly.

So when it comes to discussions across cultures, to negotiations about pricing or contracts, to innovative ideas, to being a good networker in your organisation, or to building new cross-cultural relationships, try to imagine how you would like the situation to turn out—and the chances are that it will be as you have imagined it. Then, if you focus less on 'This is what I think' and more on 'I need to be guided by you', you may well see your vision realized.

Indeed, being adopted as a good cause is not such a bad thing in our increasingly complex world of differing cultures. You will make more money and obtain better jobs with this mindset; you will create deeper friendships with new and diverse people; you will help forge fresh collaborative approaches and innovative concepts. And you will learn a comparative, open-minded approach to other people's beliefs that may develop your own spirituality and feeling for Otherness.

IT'S THE JOURNEY THAT COUNTS

So how do you get in shape for this CQ journey? What is the single most important element in your conditioning and boosting your. courage?

You notice I haven't talked about travel in itself so far, or at least not about the act of travelling. And yet many, if not all of the learning encounters I have mentioned have been in a travelling context. Or at least in the context of relocation from a usual workplace or home environment to a place where the signposts are less familiar, where it's necessary to interpret and learn how to respond to new cultural signals—and above all, to interact with people whose backgrounds may not be familiar.

Travel, of course, is meant to broaden the mind. But travel by itself is not necessarily enough to develop your cultural intelligence. It depends *how* you travel and what you take from the experience.

I may travel four times a year to Morocco or Cancun, but if I spend almost all my time at the hotel swimming pool, seeing expatriate friends for lunch and dinner, and rarely going beyond the hotel perimeter except perhaps in an organized sightseeing tour, I may return home more relaxed but with little sense that I have been somewhere completely different—or even different at all.

I have travelled like this—to the island of Phuket in Thailand, full of its expatriate enclaves and condominiums and yacht harbors. I found it difficult to experience anything of Thai daily life, or get any real sense that I was in Thailand, apart from the food in the hotel.

I am not a preacher for adventure travel, nor do I look down on those who travel just for the sake of sun, sand, and sangria with their friends. I have enjoyed holidays like this myself. However, they have done nothing for increasing my confidence in cross-cultural situations, or for exercising that extra limb or middle eye, or whatever we want to call cultural intelligence. For that—surprise, surprise—you have to interact with people from another culture, to experiment, to make mistakes, to have fun, and to generally squeeze everything you can from the world you are pitched into. Sometimes this means navigating situations you didn't expect and for which you don't have an inner guide.

You should welcome as many of these situations as possible. The longer you spend in new cultural surroundings (research suggests that more than a year in each is of the greatest benefit), the more you will benefit in terms of confidence, problem-solving, and imaginatively putting yourself in the place of others. Somehow your ear becomes attuned to other languages too, even if you don't speak them, and your inner voice listens to what other people are saying— perhaps even about you—so that you end up modifying your behaviour and *getting on better*.

This attuning to the sounds, phrases, and body language of people in other cultures is one of our deepest instincts. Perhaps it's because we don't speak the language, or very little of it, that we find ourselves observing physical signs and responding with our own bodily or facial signals, hints, expressions of warmth or warning. If we are always chatting amongst ourselves in English at the hotel swimming pool, it is unlikely that we will develop this essential part of our CQ. However, when we really travel and encounter Otherness, we learn a lot more about ourselves and about the new culture we are experiencing.

In business, this can be something as basic as not understanding why a Singaporean audience is staring at you with blank faces when you ask for questions at the end of your presentation. Or it can be discerned in the slight facial tic and impassive expression of a Chinese counterpart when asked to reply yes or no to one of your contractual questions (as posed by your interpreter). It can be heard in the odd intake of breath, like a hissing sound, a Japanese colleague might make when you discuss a business proposal.

The advice I share with my clients and audiences when faced with strange body language or unfamiliar signals like these is simple. When you travel to a new culture, act like a spy!

I don't mean you have to be Special Agent 007. I mean you should stand apart at street corners, watch how people behave, discover what makes them animated or dismissive, observe how they use gestures, find out who their friends are, see what they buy at the local market. You should wander down side streets and alleys in new cities. Find out what's going on, and if you see something that seems strange to you—perhaps an elaborate temple rite or a street festival mourning the dead—don't dismiss it. Think instead: 'Wow, this is interesting. I'd like to know how this works!' If you do volunteering work in Africa, or participate in a development aid programme in Latin America, if you take a gap year trekking through Nepal and Bhutan, if you learn Mandarin in Shanghai or Spanish in Guadalajara, the one constant should be your desire to be with people from different cultural backgrounds, and if possible, to be adopted by them as a friend and colleague.

I learned that the more experiences I had of living with friends and family in Switzerland, Italy, Hong Kong, Japan, South Korea, Singapore, Taiwan, the Philippines, the US, Australia, and Canada, the more confidence they gave me in my cultural intelligence work with businesses, CEOs, and entrepreneurs around the world.

If you want to be Bamboo Strong, you have to learn to bend like bamboo. Companies and organizations that want to expand into more diverse markets, or to effectively harness the energies of their multicultural workforce at home, need people who are confident dealing with cultural diversity.

Travel is a great generator of this confidence, especially if you know how to spy.

EYES ON THE PRIZE

While we're on the subject of travel, imagine you're standing at the entrance to one of these alleys in a new city.

Maybe you're the adventurous sort, like I now am, and maybe you're not. If you're not, how do you get yourself motivated to begin spying, and how do you put the results of that spying into action in your new business post, or development work, or educational exchange programme?

It's very easy to get discouraged when, for example, you don't speak the language, or when one particular ethnic, religious, or national group on your work team doesn't invite you to family gatherings or festivals on weekends, even though you've made every attempt to relate to them in the office.

If you're feeling lost or excluded, or simply can't find your bearings, how do you continue on your CQ journey?

My policy is to keep going down that side alley. I know that, if I do, some sort of challenge is going to turn up, something that may well intrigue me, something that will give me a simple CQ goal to achieve.

When I first arrived in Seoul, the capital of South Korea, I spent the first few days exploring the city on foot. The avenues of Seoul are extremely wide, almost Communist in their grandeur, so if I really wanted to see anything of Seoul daily life I had to get off them. I had go down one of these alleys into a neighborhood (a *dong*) where markets, and teahouses, and small stores were clustered. The alley into the *dong* would twist and turn, and I'd usually end up finding a traditional-style Korean building of wooden beams and sliding doors, with shoes left outside at the bottom of the steps to indicate there were people inside.

I found this a great challenge—and great fun. Obviously, some of these low, traditional houses were private dwellings. Others, however, had signs outside indicating food (a convex plate with something sizzling on it) or hot water (three flames rising from a sickle, which I took to be public baths).

I had learned enough about South Korea to know that foreigners were not excluded from certain inns or public baths, as they were in Japan at that time. So the way forward for me was clear. I would head down the alley to find one of these inns, or restaurants, or baths, whatever I was in the mood for, slide open the doors a little, say '*Annyeonghi-haseyo*' (I had learned 'Good day' in Korean), and see if I were welcome.

It worked! Of course, I made mistakes, but I was never chased down the street or shouted at for opening the door into someone's private living quarters. On each of the days of my first orienteering week, I chose a restaurant or a baths, somehow navigated the initial questions in my patois of simplified English and broken Korean with a few hand gestures indicating what I wanted—a drink, a meal, a locker, a towel—and settled into Korean cultural immersion for a few hours.

This was a specific challenge I gave myself for my first few days in Seoul. If all went well, the initial challenge would be followed by the reward of Korean barbecue or stone pot *bipimbap* (mixed rice), or a soak in hot thermal waters, or sometimes all three together. Believe me, it's much easier to think about your Korean cultural discoveries when your stomach is full of nutritious Korean food and your body is blissfully relaxed.

In this way, I made my first steps into learning not only the basics of the Korean language but also the basics of Korean life. Indeed, because I had discovered the pleasures of eating on a flue-heated floor at a low table, or lying out on Korean futons, or working in a simple, clean space with sliding doors and screens, I moved from my Western-style business hotel to a Korean–style, traditional inn located in one of these alleys. For the next few months, I lived a more or less traditional Korean life, with food from local restaurants delivered to my room.

And yet my first steps were small: turn left off the main avenue, try an alleyway, keep going past the private archways, stop at a sliding door with many shoes outside, listen for a conversation that sounded like restaurant diners, slide open the doors, say my Korean hello, and smile.

You can't absorb a new culture in a day, a week, or even a year. It takes time. It also takes small steps, one after the other, steps for which you can give yourself specific rewards.

If you learn to say 'Good morning or 'How are you?' in another language, that's a first step for which you should reward yourself. Learn some more, reward yourself each time. Try out some basic etiquette like presenting your business card in a formal way, bowing slightly in Japan or Korea, and raising your glass to the table and saying 'Ganpei!' ('Cheers!') before each new course in China.

If it goes well the first time, or even if it doesn't, you'll make friends just by trying, and you should celebrate. Go back to your hotel room and have a glass of wine, or go to the coffee lounge in your office building and have a coffee and some local delicacy while you read your favorite newspaper. Your goals should be small, specific, and achievable. The aim is to encourage yourself to take further steps. You should do something that makes you feel good, because that way you're much more likely to take another small step, and then another.

If you end up like me, ordering a full Korean meal from the menu with a mixture of Korean phrases and pointing at other people's plates, you will be motivated to go further— not least because of all the friends you are making, the smiles or looks of amazement from the locals in the restaurant, and the new perspectives you are gaining.

HOLDING THE REINS

Now don't get me wrong.

I'm not advocating some sort of 'go with the flow' mentality that only leads you to simply give in to whatever happens in a new country, culture, team situation, or cross-border integration meeting. The kind of small steps and cross-cultural challenges I envisage do not mean completely giving up your autonomy or your identity.

You're still going to be the foreigner when you go down that alley in an exotic new city. You're still going to be you, however much you learn another language, or practice good etiquette, or attend festivals and birthdays in a foreign country. Even when I was living in my traditional inn, eating my Korean food and speaking my basic Korean, I was under no illusion I was becoming Korean. I wasn't forgetting where I came from.

I was just becoming Me+ rather than Me-. One of the biggest stresses that expatriates have when relocating to another country or culture is of losing themselves, or rather losing their control over things, largely because they can't communicate well and don't fully understand the way things are done.

Sometimes they try to reassert control by being almost aggressively British, or American, or Australian, perhaps speaking loudly and spelling out what they mean in 'plain English', complaining that the local work colleague, or waiter, or front desk manager isn't listening properly or doesn't understand how things are done in the 'real' world.

I've seen this attitude many times, especially in the lounges of international business hotels, and it's always painful to witness. It usually comes from very tired business people who have travelled too much, are dealing with jet lag, and are clearly missing home. My Czech gym buddy Jan, who went to Melbourne from London for just one afternoon, showed me that business travel is if anything more intense now than it ever was, more demanding, and more compounded by the sheer amount of different cross-cultural encounters.

This kind of stress is further complicated by the efficiency and reach of our smart phones and devices. These ensure that we are almost always connected to our emails, our tasks, our home family life, our friends, our professional contacts, the world's news, the world's stock markets, travel advisories, and a million other subjects we think we should be aware of when we are away from home (and usually when we are at home too).

We multitask, watch television series, check Facebook and LinkedIn, send Tweets, and suffer when the Wi-Fi doesn't work or the hotel broadband is unreliable. And to all this stress is added the feeling that we are not in control of things when on a business trip or settling into a new office in another country.

Loss of control feels threatening to most people. One thing I do, whenever I arrive in a new city, is to leave my bags almost unpacked in the hotel room and go out for a walk.

It doesn't have to be a very long walk, but it does have to have an element of 'going down the alleyway' or spying about it. I once shocked my extremely well-heeled hosts from the Swiss consulate in Cairo by disappearing into the night minutes after being showed into my palatial guest room. My Swiss hosts expected to take me to a good restaurant, show me a little of the city (a discreet amount), and deliver me back so that I could retire to bed for a good rest after my flight.

When I came back from my three-hour exploration of the Medina, having discovered various bars where hookahs were smoked, located Cairo's Islamic university, and bartered for carpets for fun, my astonished hosts said I was the first and only guest that had ever gone out for a walk like that.

Okay, that was Me+, and the walk should have been shorter. But it gave me the feeling that I was in control of what I was doing. I could simply have gone around the corner and bought a newspaper by myself, and perhaps taken a local bus the next day to the Medina. Whether it's small steps, or a big impulsive breakout, it's important for stressed travellers and executives to feel they are not entirely dependent on their foreign hosts or counterparts to get around and communicate. Personally, I'm not one for guided tours of anything. But that's just me.

Planning ahead is great for developing your CQ, or rather for retaining the feeling that it's you who are holding the reins. 'Going with the flow' is also useful if you know what you are doing or what your goal is—and as long as it's you who are doing the planning.

That doesn't mean you can't listen to anyone else. Indeed, you would be foolish not to take advice from the people on the ground, but an essential part of courage is knowing what's a risk worth taking—and for that you need a sense of yourself as the one who is making the decisions.

This alleviates the stress of being in other people's hands. This is particularly the case for business people and travellers from Western cultures who are used to being independent and to working out solutions in more or less democratic forums at work.

The leaders of today, and even more so the leaders of tomorrow, will need both resilience and strength to succeed in our ever-changing and more complex world. They will need to both go with the flow and be excellent planners. Above all, they will need to be courageous. Only then will they be able to fulfill their full potential.

According to Guinness World Records, bamboos are the fastest-growing plants in the world, due to a unique rhizome-dependent system. Certain species of bamboo can grow 91 centimeters (3 feet) within a 24-hour period, at a rate of almost 4 centimeters (1.5 inches) an hour. This signifies growth of around 1 millimeter every 90 seconds, or 1 inch every 40 minutes. Bamboos have a special economic and cultural significance in South, Southeast, and East Asia, being used for building materials, as a food source, and as a versatile raw product. Bamboo has a higher compressive strength than wood, brick, or concrete, and a tensile strength that rivals steel. Little wonder that for many Chinese and other East Asians the bamboo represents perseverance or courage.

I know all about these comparative strengths because I used to chop down bamboo on my farm in the Tuscan valley to use as supports for the vines, or as tomato and runner bean canes, or even as scaffolding when the workers came to repair the outhouse where we stored the olives in November.

Every time I cut a swathe of bamboos through the large bamboo grove in my valley, I would see green shoots reappearing within a few hours. Soon those shoots were thickening and forming small bulbous growths from which further side shoots would spring.

The bamboo grove always fascinated me. It rustled like thick grass in the wind at night, bent exquisitely in different directions, and yet produced such steely supports. You had to really hack into a bamboo at an angle of forty-five degrees near to the base to have a good chance of felling it with three or four blows. But for that you needed a good sharp hatchet.

I can think of no better symbol or metaphor for the strength combined with resilience you need to develop your CQ Drive. Bamboo Strong represents the courage to tackle cross-cultural challenges, the green shoots of cultural understanding and the tolerance that will rapidly grow when you harness your desire to learn about people of other cultures.

To create your own Cultural Intelligence (CQ) Planner, with action points and strategies from this chapter, please visit www.davidcliveprice.com/planner

EXPLORATION

CQ Knowledge

CLOSE AND PERSONAL

When I was thirty-seven years old, I moved into the one-room apartment of my new partner, Simon, in a public housing estate near the old Kai Tak airport in Kowloon, Hong Kong.

This was a few weeks after I took up my new position at the international bank, when it was still too early for the salary I was earning to cover a decent rent. I had blitzed out financially in Japan writing my book, and so when I met Simon—in a group of Hong Kong Chinese friends who invited me to join them for an evening of Cantonese opera—I was still more or less broke.

I fell in love with Simon at first sight, and I was lucky that he felt the same way. So after a brief honeymoon period in the Hong Kong YMCA (yes, we knew *that* song very well), Simon suggested we live together for a while with his mother and his sister in the apartment where he had grown up.

It was only supposed to be for a few weeks, until I saved some money, but in fact I lived in the one-room apartment in Kowloon for the best part of a year until we felt secure enough to move. I don't know exactly how Simon decided that I would fit in with his family in such a tight space, but he must have felt confident because I was soon living more or less like a Hong Kong Chinese.

Simon's Ma was a typical Chinese mother. She cooked and washed not only for Simon and me but also for Simon's nephew, who she had adopted until the end of primary school, and for Simon's unmarried sister. Even though I was bigger than anyone else there, within weeks I had become a regular fixture, a subject of tolerant amusement for Simon's eight siblings and their families, who regularly visited for dinner and on weekends.

The bed on which I worked at a computer perched precariously on a breakfast table, became officially 'David's bed'. There was also a large double bed in the main room that pulled out at night for the rest of the family. The whole place was really an assortment of surfaces. Lunch and dinner were served on a collapsible table taken from out the back. Snacks, tea, and glasses were set on a low, carved table next to the votive house for the gods and ancestors.

The family always vacated the bathroom if I had to go to an appointment in a hurry, and they slowly accepted that coffee was essential to my life. Similarly, I made sure I got well out of the way when Ma or the others lit incense sticks before breakfast and again at dusk. These they placed in the various pots around the room: at the votive altar, at the outside doorway, and in front of the good-luck windmills from the temple at Wong Tai Sin. I also learnt not to take an apple from the votive pile at the altar, or to touch food being prepared for the big table set out with chicken, celery, cake, and rice on special lunar occasions like Buddha's birthday in May.

There were aspects of Simon's family life that must have surprised me when I first arrived—the mealtime anarchy of sauces and soups, of half-filled glasses and bottles, the spitting out of bones onto the table-top, the smell of fermented bean curd, the fried pig skin, the thousand-year-old preserved eggs, or the fish intestines. Soon, however, I hardly noticed.

I put it down to trust—and gratitude. Since I was accepted as a member of the family, I simply picked up what any member of the family would be doing and more or less did the same. It was another case of being adopted, this time as a kind of honorary Hong Kong Chinese. However, I doubt it would have worked if I had shown myself to be discomfited or dismissive of the way Simon's family did things.

Leaving aside the sense of Chinese family loyalty— which meant I was accepted as Simon's 'friend' without any questions asked—I was *proud* to be accepted. I was the only *gwailo* (devil man) in a sea of Chinese on the housing estate, the only Caucasian to go to the herbal medicine store and order those odd flu remedies of bitter bark and arrowroot when someone was sick, the only non-Chinese to flick through the kung fu comics at the newspaper stall or to wander in the aisles of the wet market. And although the local Chinese often stared at me, I never felt remotely threatened.

Clearly, I was enjoying myself. At the same time, I was furiously learning new things: the meaning of Chinese festivals like Lunar New Year and of giving *lai see* (lucky cash packets), of paper money being burned in a tin box on the landing as an offering at the Feast of the Hungry Ghosts, of the prosperous colour red, of the auspicious number eight, and a whole galaxy of Chinese beliefs, and rites, and ceremonies.

I was discovering new Chinese foods and ways of preparing meals. I was extending my circle of Chinese friends, enjoying old Hong Kong movies, even getting a taste for Cantonese opera (okay, not the full eight-hour version but at least excerpts with lots of drumming and martial arts). In short, I was flexing. But this time it was flexing with a difference. I probably couldn't have done any of it, or at least so easily, without my previous experience as a farmer in Italy or as a traveller in the remote parts of Japan. Later, when I wrote speeches for the Chairman and CEO of the international bank in the run-up to the handover of Hong Kong to China, or expanded my strategic consulting business into other Asian countries, I drew on my experience of Chinese daily life to create my own form of cultural intelligence.

Getting up close and personal is an essential part of this CQ knowledge. Becoming close friends with someone from another culture or background, learning all the ways you differ but also the ways you connect, refreshing your viewpoint on the world and your sense of possibilities—all are part of the same process of developing your cultural vocabulary.

No one can expect to learn all the cultures of the world. Often you need little more than a modicum of CQ knowledge for a brief meeting in Riyadh or Warsaw with a business contact—especially if you are not intending to develop operations in Saudi Arabia or Poland.

However, even for such ephemeral meetings, you need some sense of the personal, of getting behind the polite conventions to what makes your counterpart tick. You need curiosity. You also need a strong sense of how culture influences the way people think and behave, because each new encounter is building your cross-cultural confidence.

BE YOUR OWN GHQ

Cultural understanding almost always starts with the personal—which means it starts with you.

Without a strong sense of who you are and how your own culture has influenced and shaped you, you are very unlikely to know how to respond to other cultures or have the confidence to modify your behaviour in the light of your discoveries.

We are all carrying around with us our own GHQ—an individual general headquarters that has early warning procedures, listening posts in other countries, advanced intelligence gathering, and direct channels to command-and-control decision making.

If you want to be an effective player in international or multicultural contexts, you need a highly developed personal GHQ of your own. The more information your internal GHQ processes as part of your natural curiosity, the more comparative intelligence you will gather and the sharper will be your response in new situations and to new challenges. An effective GHQ begins with a strong sense of yourself and how your own culture has influenced the way you see things. Only then can you have the confidence to adapt to the people and customs and expectations of a different culture by using your CQ. I have a colleague named James, who saw action in the British army in the jungles of Malaysia, and when he retired from the army he was military attaché in various embassies in Southeast Asia. He now works as a procurement specialist for the defense industry. James is fluent in the Bahasa Malay language and has been honored for his services by the Malaysian government with the title of *Dato* (the equivalent of 'Sir').

Every time I meet James, I am impressed by his knowledge, not only of Southeast Asia in general but also by his understanding of how business works in that part of the world. He often mentions the importance of preserving 'face', or honour, in Asia and quotes as an example the British manufacturer who took months to come to a decision about a military contract with a certain Southeast Asian government. Finally, the directors of the British company attended a banquet with the government ministers responsible, and during a speech at the banquet, they abruptly announced they would not be going forward with the contract.

When the British executives left the banquet, the government minister came over to James and informed him that his government would never do business with that company again. It was not the refusal of the contract that had upset him; it was the manner in which the news was conveyed. It had caused an unpardonable loss of face. In societies that are more inclined towards the collective, where harmony, personal relationships, and respect are highly valued, such direct and 'business only' behaviour will not gain you many friends. The British company would have been better advised to couch their nonparticipation in much more conciliatory language, to offer other benefits and ways in which to work, and to have chosen a private means of communicating this to the government rather than a public event. In Asia, if a personal relationship is broken, the entire business and cultural system on which it is based collapses.

That company may have developed advanced weaponry, but it lacked the GHQ capabilities—the interpersonal confidence and respect based on an awareness of their own culture—to sell those weapons effectively. These days both individuals and organizations have to develop their own GHQ, with at least some grasp of the different business, cultural, and legal systems that exist around the world.

In addition, they should have some knowledge of differences in interpersonal values such as religious beliefs, traditions, and social etiquette. They should get a feeling for how language plays a part both verbally and nonverbally in different cultures, and they should allow themselves to be led and to have genuine curiosity. Only then can they hope to successfully manage people and relationships across cultures.

TUNE IN AND TURN ON

This does not mean that unless you study every aspect of every culture, and every cross-cultural situation, you encounter you will automatically fail!

Goodness me, don't get that idea.

You don't need a Ph.D. in anthropology or cultural studies, or to be a world-class polymath, to succeed. In fact, you don't have to speak any other language (although it helps) or have a degree.

I can quote hundreds of examples of successful leaders who have led teams in a variety of countries around the world, or from their home base, who have no specific grounding in culture or languages and yet have all the hallmarks of highly developed cultural intelligence.

Let me tell you about one of them. His name is Stefan.

I met Stefan at an event in Amsterdam celebrating the achievements of Dutch manufacturers in China, and he became my client. Stefan is the design guru for a Dutch company that makes bicycles for the global market. He spends a few months each year taking his new bicycle models on the road to various global markets including several in Asia. The first thing I learned about Stefan was his enthusiasm for each market. If he spoke about China, he raved about Shanghai noodles or the Forbidden City. If he spoke about Thailand, he praised Thai kickboxing and the Buddhist temples in Bangkok. If he talked about Brazil, he waxed lyrical about the Mardi Gras samba schools.

I discovered this local enthusiasm was echoed in the way he researched his designs for each new market his company entered. He usually went to a city in the area he chose to launch the new bicycle, such as Chiang Mai in Thailand, and visited several bicycle shops incognito before he began the design. He looked at what was for sale in the shop, the kind of bikes, the accessories, what was on the local bicycle clubs' bulletin boards, where the local cyclists went on weekends, their typical terrain and usage of their bikes. He also studied the photos and selfies of the bike owners to understand more about who they were.

Later, when his bicycle prototype was ready, he would accompany it to a launch event in, say, Osaka or Taipei, and cycle alongside the clubs he had engaged to feature the new bicycle. He offered competitions, raffles, mountain challenges, discovery trails. He socialized with the local cyclists, attended banquets, and he even invited some new owners back to Amsterdam to take part in a global launch event. In this way, every rider of his company's bikes became part of the company family. When I asked him how he communicated in each new country, he simply laughed and said, 'Just like this.' However, when I delved further, I unearthed one essential clue— the missing link to Stefan's highly powered CQ. He had lived for several years in Venezuela as a painter of advertising hoardings!

I didn't know that advertisements could be painted but apparently they could in Venezuela in days gone by. He didn't know much Spanish, he said, but he got by with his circle of Venezuelan friends, which included his Venezuelan girlfriend. He didn't have a formal degree, but he had been to art school for a short while in his teens, and this was enough to get him appointed as an advertisement artist in Venezuela.

'Just tune in and turn on,' he used to say, rephrasing Timothy Leary's counter-culture phrase on the 1960s. However, Stefan wasn't an example of the hippy culture. He was if anything a very smart and focused entrepreneur who had simply found his vocation by applying the cultural intelligence he had learned in South America to the business challenges of developing a global product for local markets. He didn't specifically study each new culture. He didn't fill himself with information or lists of etiquette and dos and don'ts. He didn't knock himself out trying to do everything perfectly. There were too many cultures involved for him to do that. Instead, he instinctively applied the CQ he had learned in his twenties in Venezuela to very specific local circumstances. His method was simple: tune in and turn on.

What makes someone like Stefan so much more of a cultural explorer than others? This is a question I often ask myself. Are those who take more risks in another culture, or who are more ready to adapt their behaviour, somehow born like that?

Perhaps some people come into the world with an extra 'third eye' that makes them more culturally adept. That could be an explanation, but then I think of the many people I have worked with. A large majority of them were not at all ready to develop their CQ at the beginning. Later, however, they became confident leaders of multicultural teams in sometimes very challenging circumstances.

So the question remains: what really raises people to a higher level of cultural knowledge and confidence? In almost every case, I think it's to do with putting yourself in another person's shoes. Or rather, it's to do with *trying on another viewpoint*. This sounds odd, but think about it for a moment. Stefan looked at those bicycle club bulletin boards for glimpses of his future customers' real lives. He wanted to know what they did—eating, drinking, enjoying themselves on weekends, competing—the festivals they attended, how close they were to their families. Then he built up a kind of identikit picture of who would buy and enjoy his bicycle.

Stefan wasn't a faceless manufacturer from the Netherlands. The photos of him launching his bicycles in China, Japan, and Thailand showed him socializing, and banqueting, and having fun with his customers. He even visited their homes, colleges, and workplaces. Cross-cultural business to him was an extension of his own life.

Looking at the world through others' eyes is both life affirming and surprising. Nowadays we are bombarded with professional, motivational, and health advice coming at us from all directions—from the Web, from digital products, from emails, from the television, from speaking events, from videos and podcasts. So it's sometimes soothing to be taken out of this well-meant onslaught of advice to a place where you can experience and observe other people's lives in tranquility.

Every time I fly between Europe and Asia, I find myself deliberately searching out the Korean movie. It's almost always subtitled and often takes place in a historical world of royal courts and warriors, naval battles, or invasions by the Chinese or Japanese. There is often a love story involved and some incredible act of heroism or compassion. I confess myself to being addicted to these Korean movies and often end up with tears rolling down my cheeks (the movies are usually beautifully made).

But the real reason I search them out is not only because I am fascinated by Koreana. It's also because they draw me into a world where I can experiment with other values and viewpoints to the ones I am used to. How would I react in this situation? What's the difference between the way this Korean family behaves in a crisis and how my own might behave? Would the reactions of the hero be considered right or wrong in my world? Would I choose love or filial duty?

At the height of thirty thousand feet, closed off in my hermetic dark space, I am lost in another culture to the one I know—and this time I don't have to worry about how my reactions or behaviour might look to someone from that culture. I am simply, and soothingly, an observer.

It's the same with novels. You don't have to be a language freak to enjoy novels from other languages and cultures. I once tried to read Joyce's *Ulysses* in the French edition (my advice: don't!). However, you should try and enjoy the literature of other countries in translated versions. I can think of no better guide to the way a culture influences characters in relation to their family, loves, friends, dreams, and aspirations than, say, Haruki Murakami's depiction of Japanese society in his novels or Gabriel García Márquez's magical realist evocation of Latin America. You can go as high or low brow as you want—as long as the novel gives you a refreshing viewpoint on a whole new world.

The same applies to plays, art, and even operas. The subjective works of individual artists do not necessarily give a rounded picture of a society, but often the works of a group of artists—such as the Viennese Secession school of the late nineteenth century, which produced the paintings of Gustav Klimt and Otto Wagner—tell you more about their world and the state of their culture than a hundred history books. Go to any city in the world and look at the architecture.

What does it tell you about the culture? Is it neo-classicist like Baron Haussmann's Paris or monumental and defiant like Seoul? Then visit an art museum or gallery. You will soon gain greater knowledge not only about the society's traditions, beliefs, and social structure but also about contemporary reflections of those beliefs and ideas.

I couldn't have understood the life and culture of the Italian courts and city states in the late Renaissance without reference to Da Vinci, Michelangelo, Mantegna, Titian, Veronese, Giulio Romano, and many others. When I finished studying and went to live in what seemed to be one of those artists' cypress-and-olives landscapes, I met numerous country versions of the nobles and courtesans, engineers and apprentices the famous court artists had depicted.

You can also learn a lot about Italy from the plots of Verdi operas, or about the history of China from Beijing or Cantonese operas. I discovered a great deal about Burmese belief in spirits and the role of Buddhism in daily life from watching Burmese puppet plays and Burma's extraordinary live *pwe* or musical dramas.

The most revealing film about my life in Switzerland, and of the difference between the Swiss approach to death and my own society's, was a film called *Rosie—A Man, His Lover, and His Mother*, which I recently downloaded straight to my television. After it finished, I greedily devoured a historical drama about a woman assassin in Tang dynasty China by Hou Hsiao Hsien, a famous Taiwanese director. We have all the world's cultures around us at the press of a button—all we have to do is search them out.

EMPIRE OF THE CUISINES

If the way to a man's heart is through his stomach, then the way to everyone's CQ is down the same route. The process of globalisation, rapid travel, and 24/7 connectivity has brought the different cuisines of the world, and the cultures that created them, much closer to our everyday life. When I was a young man in Britain in the 1960s and 1970s, the national cuisine was a monocultural, 'meat and veg' sort of thing. I remember my excitement to be taken to a Bengali restaurant in central London from my suburban south London town and finding the whole experience (mixed with a visit to the theatre to see *The Merchant of Venice*) incredibly exotic.

Even in Cambridge, the only foreign food available was in a curry house at the back of my college and a Greek moussaka place in Green Street. It was a big effort to find an espresso bar in London, and the bewildering range of coffee choices (pistachio and rose mocha, anyone?) now available in every coffee bar would have been unimaginable.

Nowadays, when I watch UK *MasterChef* on television, I find myself struggling to recognize some of the ingredients from cuisines all over the world, often fused together artfully on one plate for a particular course: Lebanese, Chinese, Japanese, Korean, Caribbean, Polish, Italian, French, and many more. The confidence with which the competing amateur chefs handle Japanese fish roe, or Indian sambal, or Malaysian coconut and lime leaves makes my eyes—and especially my mouth—water. No longer do you have to take yourself to Paris for fine dining. The cuisines of the world are available in cities from Singapore and Tokyo to London, from Buenos Aires to New York and Los Angeles. And it's not only fine dining. Street versions and family versions (the Italian *cucina della mamma*) are available too. As our cities become more and more of a multicultural hot pot, we are learning more about different cultures of the world through what the people of those cultures eat, where they find it, how they prepare it, how they eat it, and how they reflect on it. If we are what we eat, it's pretty clear we are becoming ever more multicultural.

This has big implications for our cultural knowledge. The first benefit for our CQ is that when we try out a new cuisine, or new dishes within that cuisine, we are in effect flexing. We are asking ourselves to step over into some other taste region—maybe unfeasibly spicy, maybe cooked in a strange wine or paste, maybe featuring meats, or fish, or vegetables that we have never tried before. The point is that we are experimenting, taking a bold leap of faith (can *you* tolerate a red Thai curry?), and some part of us is probably also wondering how the inhabitants of this country—Slovenia, the Maldives, Peru—came up with this dish.

That's because cuisine is in many ways culture.

A couple of decades ago, I published a book on Korean cuisine together with the chefs of the Shilla Hotel in Seoul. They provided the recipes, the public relations department provided the fantastic photos of each dish, and I provided the essays on South Korea's different regions, how the dishes developed, and their historical and cultural background.

What do you think when you hear the words Korean food? You probably go straight to the stereotype: meat barbecue. Koreans eat a lot of meat, so their main dish is spicy grilled beef, right?

Wrong. It's true that the Koreans are descended from Mongol horsemen who hunted animals on the steppes of Russia and in China. The Mongols sliced up their prey on concave metal shields, which they held over open wood fires. And so to this day Koreans eat barbecued meat—but that is by no means all that they eat.

Much of their cuisine is vegetarian, consisting of fermented spicy cabbage (*kimchi*) and an array of small dishes containing varieties of mountain roots, grasses, herbs, and spices. These dishes emerged as the staple of Korean cuisine when Chinese Confucian beliefs took over from Buddhism as the main influence on the royal court. The king banished the Buddhist monks to their mountain monasteries, and there they lived on a vegetarian diet of grasses, vegetables, and roots gathered in the nearby vicinity.

So if you really want to enjoy Korean cuisine, it pays to find out a little more about Korean culture. That will enable you to choose the authentic Korean dishes in a restaurant that may well offer barbecued beef (and little else) on a menu intended for Western eyes. However, if you look around, you will see local Koreans being served numerous side dishes of vegetables, roots, and *kimchi*. Korean food would be much duller without them.

The same is true of every cuisine in the world. The more we enjoy them as passports to other cultures, the more we develop our readiness to enjoy new experiences and build new relationships.

If you want to succeed in business in many parts of the world, such as Asia, you have to be ready to socialize over food. In China, for example, there are elaborate traditions of banqueting (at least eight courses, eleven for a VIP). Business is not the main item on the menu, but food definitely is. If you can try odd Chinese dishes as I have done— chrysalis of silkworm comes to mind—and continue smiling as you discreetly place a morsel at the side of your rice bowl, you will be accepted as a potential business partner.

The discussion and tasting of food in Asia is the single most important factor in building a long-term business relationship. If you can talk food, and try a little of everything, you're in. If you stick with knife and fork and ask for sausages, you're out.

I had a German aunt who lived in the San Barnaba district of Venice—or rather David had a German aunt, and I kind of adopted her because she was like someone out of a novel.

She was very old and had come to Venice during the Second World War, escaping from the Nazis and hiding herself away in this forgotten corner of this forgotten island. She was very proud of her Swabian (southwest German) heritage, and the Swabian dialect she spoke, and also of her ability to converse with the local Venetians in their colorful language.

Speaking Venetian dialect came in handy because she always had some problem with her crumbling mini-palazzo by the edge of the canal, with its funny turreted tower that tended to lose bricks at odd moments, and she could call on the local Venetian firemen to do repairs. Aunt Itte always fascinated me with her tribe of cats and a cigarette permanently clamped between her lips. I don't know how she survived financially because she didn't seem to have ever had a proper job but was rather a lady of *belles lettres*.

I spent endless hours at her kitchen table in San Barnaba, hearing the rain dripping from the turrets, sipping the extremely strong Negronis she made, and listening to her speak of Thomas Mann's *Magic Mountain* or Marcel Proust's *À la recherche du temps perdu*. She had a way of looking at me quizzically when she asked a question—which was inevitably deep and searching—and of waiting for my answer with cigarette poised and deep eyes narrowing.

One day, she asked me what language I was going to learn next.

I was silent for a while. I was very proud of having picked up some Swiss German, and now I could more or less speak fluent Italian, so I couldn't imagine starting another language.

Seeing my reluctance to reply, she said, 'Each new language is a window on the world.'

I looked at her for a moment, and she looked at me and slowly, very slowly, tilted her head to one side.

'Okay, okay,' I said, conceding defeat. 'I will learn some Japanese.'

As usual, Aunt Itte had gotten right to the point. She foresaw that in my peripatetic life around the world I would need more than just two languages. I would have to become like her: living in her Venetian enclave and speaking her Venetian dialect, Swabian German, English, French, and Spanish. She may have been overstating my ability, but she knew I was willing to learn.

Language and culture are entwined. Language helps you understand the norms and assumptions of a particular culture, its underlying beliefs, its way of looking at and shaping situations, peoples, and aspirations. At the same time, culture helps to explain and contextualize language as well as infuse it with nonverbal signals, tacit understandings, and the vital subtext to any conversation.

For example, a Chinese might tell me that top football teams in the English Premier League always seem to be 'tiger head and snake's tail'. He is suggesting in his use of Chinese metaphor that the tendency of British sporting heroes to collapse in a heap after every triumph and lose the next match is akin to how two-headed animals might behave in their zodiac.

He is giving me a worldview, a hint as to his own nation's more tough and realistic approach to challenges, and a quick lesson in Chinese astrological belief. He is also perhaps making an allusion to his country's rapid economic rise followed by inevitable economic and social adjustments.

Language is innately colorful and rich in sayings and allusions that give you vital clues as to how that person ticks or that society works. It is also, quite simply, a way of getting in and getting on. If you have a few stock phrases of politeness and enquiry in Japanese, Thai, Russian, or Spanish, the chances are that you will be more warmly welcomed in those cultures than if you stiffly bark in English. Indeed, in this age of virtual global teams and emails that are entirely bereft of the usual body language, expressions, or smiles, a few phrases in the language of your correspondent—even if you usually communicate in simplified English—is a sure way of smoothing out difficult decisions or thorny questions.

Yes, Aunt Itte, language is a window on the world.

It's extraordinary how instinctive it is too. When I chat in Italian with my barista Fabrizio in the gym lounge, I often find myself unconsciously using Italian hand gestures to accompany the cadences of what I am saying. A certain gesture with the thumb, forefinger, and middle finger of my right hand, joined together and extending almost horizontally from the elbow with my right shoulder hunched, expresses 'What are these people thinking?' or 'What the hell is going on here?' just as clearly as saying it in words. In fact, you can often use the gestures in place of the words.

Language is linked to culture through facial expressions and gestures, just as much as through allusions and tone. I recently heard an Anglo-French cultural expert ask his audience who—apart from the English themselves—

understood the ironic subtext of British English, the understatement (which often means the opposite of what the British are saying), the elaborate but double-edged politeness. The consensus among the audience was that you could only really understand it by reading body language and facial hints allied to tone.

In other words, Aunt Itte's view of language as a window on the world also allows you to see into the heart of a culture, including its nonverbal expressions.

VALUES VERSUS STEREOTYPES

But not even art, or cuisine, or language will help you develop your CQ knowledge if you simply use whatever you learn to bolster your preconceived stereotypes of a culture. There's a big difference between discovering more about a society's predominant values and making those values serve pre-existing 'types' in your mind.

For example, if you have an *idée fixe* that the Japanese tend to be unreadable, hierarchic in their work structures, and unfriendly to foreigners bordering on the xenophobic, you are not going to make much headway in developing cross-cultural relationships with the Japanese. The same applies if you think all Mediterranean peoples are lazy because they have a long siesta during the day. Everything you then learn about Mediterranean peoples will go to support your stereotype. That would be a pity because you would miss the important values siestas promote. These include avoiding the heat of the day to work better in the later afternoon and evening, preserving work–life balance and a healthy lifestyle, and being able to conduct business as a gracious preliminary to dinner, where relationships can be better developed.

For every culture we tend to have a set of expressed or secret stereotypes: Americans in your face, Chinese corrupt, French hypocritical, British condescending, Germans coldly efficient, Indonesians time wasting, Russians bullying. These stereotypes tend to be reinforced by the values identified as belonging to particular cultures or groups of cultures in the cross-cultural resources you may have come across—such as a cross-cultural studies book, a cultural training course, or a global leadership seminar.

What kind of values?

In your training or book you might learn that some countries like the US or Australia emphasize the rights and responsibilities of the individual, while others like China are more collectivist, focusing on personal relationships and the benefits of the group more than individual goals. You might be told that some cultures like Britain and Hong Kong have a higher tolerance for risk and ambiguity than Japan or Russia, where planning and reliability are emphasized rather than unpredictable situations. Cooperation and family or relationships are more highly prized in Chile and the Netherlands than in more competitive and assertive cultures like Hungary and Japan.

However, such values as demonstrated in these often very helpful resources are only guidelines. They are useful to develop CQ as long as you recognize that there are many individual exceptions and gradations along the way. Cross-cultural studies help us to understand that cultures differ. However, it is also important to note that CQ Knowledge can only be truly developed in relation to individuals, not entire cultures.

WHO ARE YOU ANYWAY?

I've lived and worked in so many different countries and cultures around the world, I might be forgiven for thinking I am an inhabitant of Thomas More's Nowhere—or rather Everywhere.

But that would be untrue. I'm as much a product of my own background and upbringing as anyone else. There are various cultural influences that have shaped me: an Anglo-Welsh childhood, a grammar school in the Home Counties, several years of study and research at Cambridge University, a Swiss partner and life in a multicultural country, my Italian rural community, the gay subculture of New York, the corporate culture of the international bank in Hong Kong, and so on.

It would be easy to assume from these influences that my cultural identity is all over the place. However, I'm glad to say it isn't. I feel very much part of my time and background. It wasn't always like this. There was a time when I rejected my background and culture, when I felt that the Britain I had been brought up in was full of prejudice and class distinction. I wanted to escape from being a Cambridge academic, a privileged white male, a 'colonial' English type, a product of the class system, and above all from being what I considered a prisoner of sexual prejudice and discrimination.

Perhaps I was right to avoid or reject these aspects of my own culture at the time, and this tendency was encouraged by the new cultural viewpoints I gained in other countries. But as I've grown older, I've learned to accept the good and the bad in my own background and tried to understand more what has made me who I am. In many ways, I'm proud that I can marry my partner in my own country, and that all my experiences as a minority or an outsider have given me much deeper insight into cross-cultural dilemmas and challenges. My experience of not being aligned with my own culture has allowed me to see the conflicts and tensions in other cultures. It has enabled me to approach those dilemmas and solve those clashes for other people in my cross-cultural work around the world.

If we don't understand ourselves or our own culture, we are unlikely to understand others.

YOU ARE NOT I

Of course, knowing how we are shaped by our own culture does not mean we should actively seek to impose it on others. If we think our culture is the *only* way, the *best* way, the *right* way to do things, we lose our comparative sense and place major obstacles in the way of developing true cultural knowledge.

How often have I heard business people say in foreign countries, 'This is the way we usually do it,' or 'Don't they get how to do things properly around here?'

Being confident of your own culture does not mean being dismissive of others. Indeed, I often think that those same business travellers might be surprised if their local Chinese, or Indian, or Brazilian counterpart turned round and said, 'This is the way *we* do it!' The best way to get around this arrogance is to realize that there are a multiplicity of possible viewpoints. Just because someone looks like you, even sounds like you, they do not necessarily think like you. It's important to get used to this idea. I often try reading a story—say about the Hong Kong student demonstrations against lack of participation in democratic elections—in the *South China Morning Post* (Hong Kong's daily), in the *China Daily* (the official mouthpiece of the Chinese government), and in *The Times* of London. I'm amazed how the same story can be reported in different ways according to varying cultural and political viewpoints.

I tune in to the BBC News (London), Channel News Asia (Singapore), and also Al Jazeera (Qatar) for developments about conflicts in the Middle East and migration crises in Europe; these stories are reported very differently. I also get a feeling for different positions watching both Fox News and CNN for coverage of domestic American politics and world news. Some of the commentary may irritate me like hell, but I try to keep calm. I can always learn from the different angles.

The same applies to religious attendance. Although I am an agnostic Christian with a tendency towards Buddhism, that doesn't stop me finding out about other people's beliefs and studying other religious observances. I have visited Christian churches, Islamic mosques, Buddhist temples, Jewish synagogues, and Hindu shrines. I have gone to feminist meetings as the only male present and have been made to feel welcome (by some members, if not all). I have gone to Christian fundamentalist meetings where the agenda was against gay and lesbian marriage.

It didn't change my own beliefs. However, I may have modified them while listening to other people's views. At the very least I found out what made other people tick, and I always learned something new.

The world is too complex to view it in black and white or to be assured that your way is the right or only way. Every time I listen to a debate on Europe and migration now, or read an in-depth report from a newspaper of opposing loyalties on the political spectrum, I find myself changing my viewpoint and convictions—or at least modifying them. One day I am persuaded that being part of the European Union and deferring to Schengen's open-borders policy is right, and the next day I am ready for Britain's exit from the European Union to seek greater opportunities in the world and control our own borders from mass migration.

This is what it means to be informed citizens in a multicultural world. We can change our viewpoints. Above all, based on our willingness to listen and learn, we can have different viewpoints—sometimes at the same time.

THE KARATE KID'S MENTOR

There was a movie I was fond of watching on television when I lived in my One Room in Kowloon.

It was called *The Karate Kid,* and it ran quite frequently on the Chinese channels. Sometimes the TV trailer showed a black-and-white still of a scene from the movie. It depicted a white-haired Japanese karate instructor called Mr. Miyagi, who was shown demonstrating the correct karate moves to a tall American adolescent he was coaching to fight back against the small-town bullies who had pursued him all his life.

For some reason that movie image stuck in my mind: the older and the younger man standing in a sort of frozen t'ai chi pose, gathering the energy of the universe with their palms extended upwards and their knees half bent. I loved the harmony of the image, perhaps because I saw my Chinese neighbors doing similar t'ai chi exercises every morning in the housing estate car park. I also loved the quote in capital letters that appeared below the image of the Karate Kid:

IT'S OK LOSE TO OPPONENT, MUST NOT LOSE TO FEAR—MR MIYAGI.

These ungrammatical English words seemed to perfectly capture the meaning of courage and also the importance of training in preparation for whatever big step you are taking into the unknown.

In today's multicultural world, those steps are increasingly required—not necessarily to beat the bullies, but to have the inner strength and confidence to take on cross-cultural challenges, to persevere against the odds, and ultimately to win. Along the way, you may well LOSE TO OPPONENT. You may make mistakes. You may be beaten by the competition. But the overall message remains true: if you have a mentor and guide, you will be able to overcome irrational fears and inner doubts.

When I started out in Hong Kong, I was very lucky. I had a mentor at my side almost immediately: Simon, or rather Simon, his family, and friends. They showed me how to enjoy Chinese life and to learn so many things about myself in this new culture without feeling that I was undergoing a training course (although there's nothing like a partner to correct you when you choose the wrong set of chopsticks to eat your rice).

However, I would not have thought of Simon as a guide for how to handle the corporate world of the international bank. For that, I needed someone who could show me how the bank functioned, the right way to handle the pecking order, how to get the ear of the Chairman or CEO without putting them and me in an awkward position, how to write speeches for multicultural audiences and different countries or organizations, and a thousand other topics.

In my first weeks of induction, I was assigned an expatriate with long experience in the bank's public relations department. He was very good at the professional aspects of his job, but there was one problem. I soon discovered that he was very poor in handling both his Chinese staff and his expatriate deputy, a young and very bright Englishwoman who had lived in Denmark. In fact, he was well known as one of the office bullies.

So after my first weeks of induction, I tactfully removed myself from his mentorship. I chose instead a Chinese woman whom I had made friends with on my very first day. Cindy was the perfect choice: a fairly senior manager, poised and articulate. In the following months and years she helped me navigate the cross-cultural barriers within the bank, kept me informed of the latest news on the Chinese and expatriate grapevine (not always the same thing), and generally coached me in Chinese business etiquette and corporate behaviour.

I have lived in many countries around the world, and in all of them I have had a mentor and guide. Sometimes they have been locals, sometimes they have been expatriates, and sometimes I have used a mixture of the two to maintain a balanced perspective. In New York, an African-American painter guided me through the gay underground—including showing me S&M bars that later made a short appearance in *Alphabet City*. Leon had a healthy skepticism about the conventions and attitudes of the gay world. He was my friend and mentor whenever I was lost or confused (and I often was). He also taught me a great deal about living between and within two cultures: the African-American experience, and what the novel's narrator calls 'the whole white Anglo-Saxon caboodle of work, free market, poor to the wall, virtue.'

I didn't know it at the time, but Leon was my coach in New York, offering me helpful guidelines and interpretations of what was going on in this *mélange* of cultures, races, and minorities. It helped that he was just as much at home at an arts soirée on the Upper East Side of Manhattan as he was in the warren of bars in the meatpacking district near the River Hudson or in the artists' ateliers of SoHo. Leon was a super-cool mentor.

Whoever you choose to be your coach, mentor, or guide, make sure that they are giving you objective advice and guidance. Sometimes those who live too closely to their own culture cannot stand back from it and view it as a foreigner might see it. In this sense, expatriates are very helpful if they have a sensitive understanding—rather than a resentful intolerance—of the culture in which they (and you) find themselves.

But in my view, expatriates are only the first step. If you really want support and guidance, you have to find someone with professional experience across a variety of cultures. They need to be familiar with your own national culture and, ideally, with your sector or industry culture too. They will help you focus on what is different or special about the cross-cultural environment you are encountering, whether at home or overseas. They will have strong awareness of Otherness and of themselves in culturally diverse situations. And they will ask the kind of questions that allow you to discover a new culture by yourself—and the kind of barriers you will have to navigate—rather than instructing you.

When I took over the abandoned farm in the hills of Tuscany, I had a close friend and co-worker in the person of Parise. He seemed to come with the farm, the last in a long line of *mezzadri,* or tenant farmers who cultivated the land for a share of the crops. Parise and his wife Leda (everyone in that landscape seemed to have mythological names), were my mentors and guides.

He showed me how to climb inside the olive tree and clean out the blackened branches that had grown entangled in the center of the tree, allowing the olive to breathe again. He encouraged me to prune the garlands of olive leaves so that they hung down the outside of the plant, giving the tree its distinctive wine-glass shape and making it a healthy bearer of olives in season. He also showed me how to harvest the olives in November, using a ladder and a wicker basket hung at my side to strip the garlands of their fruit.

This was just one aspect of Tuscan life he unveiled for me. There were many others: how to prune the vines, how to support them with bamboo, how to bind them with cypress. Parise showed me how to grow potatoes, zucchini, tomatoes, beans, and artichokes, and Leda helped me cook them. Both of them showed me how to covertly ignore the demands of the visiting Florentine landlord (who owned one wing of the house) in a centuries-old tradition of tenant farmer resistance, so that he could not bully me.

We shared a great deal, my mentors and I, in our little Tuscan valley. But the one thing that Parise always said when I was learning was, '*non per insegnarvi, Davide*' ('not to teach you, David'). Everything I learned from him was prefaced with this phrase. Somehow he knew that instructing me would do me no good. I would forget or ignore the lesson. However, whatever I discovered by being guided by him would stay with me forever.

And indeed it has.

A recent research study by the global human resource consultancy, Development Dimensions International, showed that global CEOs believe cultural intelligence to be one of the top critical skills they want leadership teams to have. The same study revealed that only 34 percent of global leaders surveyed ranked working with people from different cultures as a true strength.

A good coach and mentor will help you ask the important questions of yourself and others. They will not teach you but rather guide you, so that you stand a much better chance of joining that top third of global leaders who are truly Bamboo Strong.

To create your own Cultural Intelligence (CQ) Planner, with action points and strategies from this chapter, please visit www.davidcliveprice.com/planner

PERSPECTIVE

CQ Strategy

FOOLS RUSH IN

I have a Jewish-American composer friend who used to visit us in Switzerland, and on one occasion he came down to the farm in Italy.

Frank is a lovely and highly intelligent man, with wide experience of travelling the world and, of course, working with people from many different backgrounds for his Broadway shows and musicals. If there was one person I could think of as having both the drive to understand cultural differences (CQ Drive) and the broad knowledge of how people behave differently in other cultures (CQ Knowledge) it is Frank. He has even written musicals that portray the clash and partial resolution of these differences in thrilling and inspiring form.

However, when he came to Switzerland—and later to Italy—it always intrigued me that the usually sharp-witted Frank was slightly off beam in the quick conclusions he drew from what he saw.

In Zürich, for example, Frank would be puzzled when he met a new group of Swiss people, each one of whom would take time to shake his hand and introduce themselves formally by giving their surnames, and expect him to do the same. Frank always introduced himself with his Christian name. He also rarely shook hands, preferring a pleasant smile and perhaps a joke to break the ice.

Seeing his hosts looking slightly uncomfortable with this manner of introduction, Frank immediately assumed that the

Swiss were overly formal and 'Germanic'. I told him this was not the case: the hand-shaking and offering of surnames were just a Swiss way of showing healthy democratic respect for everyone present—not an example of Prussian coldness. But I'm not sure Frank was ever convinced.

It was the same when he visited our Tuscan valley. Frank used to observe that Parise and Leda and other of our farmer neighbors regularly left baskets of fresh vegetables and flowers outside our door at the end of the day. Sometimes they even hung a skinned, cleaned, and partially chopped rabbit in a plastic bag on a nail near the doorbell (out of reach of any interested dogs or cats).

He concluded from this that our neighbors would call in our debt to them at some future date. So much free produce, he reasoned, could not possibly come without some sort of strings attached.

Again, I had to explain to him that the giving of fresh vegetables was a normal reflex on the part of neighbours living in a communal, natural setting. We exchanged whatever we had that was extra to our needs because that was the way of the Italian countryside at the time. You never knew what natural emergency could come along (we had severe snow one winter that blighted many of our olive trees). Being bound in mutual obligation to help each other out was an essential aspect of survival. It also meant that the good stuff didn't go to waste.

However, try telling a seasoned New Yorker that gifts can be quite innocent and without obligation.

He was once standing beneath the loggia at the entrance to the farmhouse when one of our neighbors came by with a bundle of freshly cut artichokes and a basket of figs. I could hear Frank talking to the farmer and a disjointed discussion unfolding, in English and Italian, until I came along to smooth the whole thing over.

It wasn't Frank's fault. His city environment made him suspicious of unearned gifts. As I moved around the world to places where I didn't feel as safe as I did in the Italian countryside, I caught echoes of Frank's suspicions in my own reactions. In countries as diverse as Burma, the Philippines, Brazil, and Egypt, I assumed from very little evidence that I was being taken for a ride or being put into an awkward position by little gifts that simply came from the heart—gifts that were tokens of community and friendship rather than time bombs of responsibility.

At such moments, I also rushed in with my assumptions—even though I was armed with plenty of CQ Drive and CQ Knowledge. Instead of standing back a moment and reflecting on what I was being offered, or on the *way* it was being offered, I jumped to conclusions.

I suspect this is something everyone is tempted to do when they are travelling. If you don't know a country or a culture and are visiting for the first time, you are very quick to see things that can give you cultural clues to what is going on. It's just a short step from this to arriving at conclusions without noticing that we are simply feeding our preconceptions.

I remember my first visit to Seoul. I had been told that South Korea was a very Confucian society where men tended to dominate both in the family and in business. I could understand this because I had studied some Korean history and culture (as I mentioned in Part 3). I knew from my reading how deeply rooted Confucian belief was in Korean life and society, with Confucianism arriving at the royal court from China a thousand years ago.

So every time I saw a man taking the lead in a Seoul business meeting with other women managers present, or a man walking a few steps ahead of his wife and children in the Seoul subway, I ticked a box in my head that read 'Confucian' or 'typical Korean male'.

You can therefore imagine my surprise when I went to a family dinner in a private house in Seoul, a rare honour for a foreigner. I found the male head of the family cooking in the kitchen, carrying dishes in and out to the table, and being soundly told off by his wife in front of everyone for forgetting some ingredients at the supermarket on his way home.

Little by little, I discovered that my little Korean knowledge was a dangerous thing. It had encouraged me to rapidly apply my cultural learning without noticing the lack of connection between what I knew intellectually and what was facing me in reality. South Korean men may have played the role of patriarchs in public, but at home it was the women who were in charge and—as I soon discovered—also ran the household finances.

This is where Perspective or CQ Strategy comes in. It's not enough to be highly motivated to learn, or to have acquired cultural knowledge. You must also strategize how to apply that understanding in action. This often means reflecting upon what you experience in an unfamiliar culture, and holding off your assumptions until you have time to analyze and possibly adjust your behaviour to what is in front of you. In our incredibly fast-paced world where time is money, this deeper thought process is sometimes very difficult to achieve. But without CQ Strategy— or a plan of action— our CQ Drive and CQ Knowledge are often unhelpful, or worse, dangerous.

BIG PICTURE PAINTING

Of course, standing back and reflecting is often easier said than done—especially when we travel or are faced by new cultural challenges.

It's very tempting to jump to conclusions about why that person is dressed that way, or why they eat those kinds of things, or why they talk so loudly, or why they are not queuing in a proper line. We do it all the time when we are confronted with something new.

However, when you are rugby-scrummed out of the way on the Seoul subway, shoe-horned into the Tokyo metro, trampled in the bus queue in Shanghai, or swept aside in the rush for the train in Mumbai, remember that the bigger picture counts much more than little details. And it often clarifies.

You have to ask *why* something is like that, rather than dismissing it with a ready-made prejudice. I can think of many situations on Western transport systems that aren't ideal but where the sheer weight of numbers or pressure to survive in very tight spaces is less than in Korea, China, Japan, or India. It's often helpful to reflect how we might behave if we were regularly caught up in such situations. Would we be better or worse mannered than the stoic citizens of those densely populated countries?

We all have different levels of tolerance, and we all have different ways of thinking about what is right and wrong. If you're quick to judge, you're probably not good at seeing the bigger picture. Every cross-cultural situation in which we find ourselves has elements of difference to what we are used to and therefore can be quickly pigeonholed. How often do we say 'That's not right', when we have no comparison or benchmark against which to measure our assumed category of right or wrong?

Leaders of companies and organizations are increasingly being asked to see the bigger picture as they interact with customers, suppliers, colleagues, and teams from many different backgrounds and cultures. Those who only see the details have their place in the multicultural work environment. However, it is the big-picture thinkers who stand back and say, 'That's curious. I've never seen that before. I wonder how that works,' who are leading their organizations into new realms of creativity and innovation.

Just as in every aspect of life, the aha moments occur when you stand back for a minute, when you leave the details alone entirely and digest them unconsciously. This is what happens when you take your new cultural knowledge and reflect, avoid judgment, and eventually synthesize what you have experienced into a new and deeper understanding of how that culture works—and how you stand in relation to it.

That is how Perspective, or CQ Strategy, works.

My plan of action in South Korea was simple—I was going to write a series of business and travel essays for an American Express magazine (and collect them together for a book, which I later called *Phoenix Rising: A Journey Through South Korea*). As part of my strategy, I was scheduled to visit a large island off the southern coast of Korea called Cheju or the 'Honeymooners' Isle'. The rich volcanic landscapes of Cheju were suitable as backdrops for wedding pictures, and the island's hot-spring resorts also attracted a large number of international business conventions.

I decided to take a train from the capital city of Seoul down through the spine of South Korea to the port of Wando on the south coast, where a ferry would take me across a short stretch of the Yellow Sea to Cheju City. My plans for the excursion unfolded perfectly: an efficient ticket system at Seoul station, orderly queuing at the platform for the train, allocated seating, a relatively tranquil journey through the tea plantations and mountain passes of Kwangju province, and finally arrival at noon on the southern coast.

Boarding the ferry at Wando was also seamless—hardly any pushing, polite faces and smiles all around. What a pleasure to travel in such an ordered society, I thought. Other societies could well learn from the Land of the Morning Calm: a peaceful society in which people more or less know their place in the hierarchy, and good behaviour, respect, and harmony are the norm.

As the boat shunted backwards from the quay, I took up my seat on one of the upper decks. All around me I could see huge parties of people on their weekend outings, covering every bit of the open deck with their bags and bodies, removing their slippers, some already sleeping full-length as if poleaxed by slumber where they stood. I might have been on a refugee boat somewhere except for the complete absence of noise. I only witnessed one brief argument, between an old mother and her son, in the surrounding mass of bodies.

However, just as the boat began to weave its way out of the harbor, something changed in the atmosphere. A reed pipe began to play. Someone began to beat a drum, and then a cymbal. Those somnolent bodies stirred and sat up, playing cards appeared, alcohol, soft drinks, picnic snacks, wood-piece games, and soon I was being offered food and drink from all quarters by women and men anxious that a foreigner should not be left out of the proceedings.

It was the women who really began the party. I suspect the men would have been happy enough in their own circles, clapping their hands and waving their hats, or betting with miniature cards, but sticking to their own kind. The women were undoubtedly the agents provocateurs (they were playing the drums). It was they, and particularly the older ones in their traditional clothes of pink and mauve silks, their hair wrapped in a tight bun, who began to make little pirouettes as the clapping went on, and then great circular motions reminiscent of the traditional Korean farmers' dance, their hands above their heads acting as drum beats.

Suddenly, the whole deck seemed to be whirling gaily—until there was a whistle, and the ship's officers came by and looked sternly at the passengers. Again the women were the most successful in quelling the mutiny. Temporarily. Perhaps it was feared that the ship would go down in a kind of stamping frenzy.

Not that the old ones seemed to mind a bit. Soon they were encouraging everyone back onto their feet. And, of course, it had to happen that, tired of my snappy camera, they invited the only foreigner to take part, waving and pawing at me as the clapping grew more insistent, and the guttural voices began their Indian-type wailing. I had no choice. Before the astonished eyes of the ship's intervening crew, I was wheeling absurdly to the encouragement of two women who could be my mother, but who behaved as if they were at a hippy gathering of the 1960s.

Nor was the dancing wild in the meaning of frenzied. Despite being loud, the whole performance was focused and musical, an organized spontaneity, and not without its childlike side, as every now and then the officers returned to make us sit down.

Perhaps it was the defiance of the women. Perhaps it was the older generation—the generation of the Korean War—taking the lead and acting like youngsters. But suddenly my whole idea of life in South Korea changed.

The captain sat in his open cabin entertaining chosen visitors wearing white socks, while we were intermittently chided and pushed, before ribbing each other back into ululating motion. All like children. The old women even pouted like children before starting up again, while over in the corner a respectable, grinning man underwent an attempted debagging at the hands of another group of women. People fell heavily to the ground in the mêlée. No one was hurt. No one complained. On my first excursion in Korean waters, a rough-and-tumble seemed entirely appropriate.

Later, I wrote all this down in my diary—including my thoughts about it, which is why I can reproduce the scene in such detail here.

TUNING YOUR RADAR

I keep a diary or notebook almost everywhere I go, especially when I travel. I find it calming to have somewhere private where I can record my thoughts, impressions, concerns, and above all where I can think about the characters I meet (and who may end up in one of my books).

I started this habit in Italy, when I was attempting to understand aspects of Italian rural life, and I continued when I travelled through the interior of the country, visiting

Etruscan towns like Tarquinia that were similar to my home base of Volterra with their rich history and agrarian traditions. I spent a few days in each location, noting, comparing, storing information, and analyzing casual encounters.

Wherever I went, from Crotone in the deep south to the cave dwellings of Matera, from Naples to Sicily, I kept a diary. In this journal, I made notes about the people I met, their passions and beliefs, as well as aspects of their lives that I needed more time to think about, such as their sometimes fanatical Catholicism, their penchant for blood feuds, their unexpected kindness to strangers, and their *campanilismo* (deep attachment to local roots).

When I look back over those diaries and notebooks now, I see that they are often full of misunderstandings I had to get off my chest—rants about perceived slights by shopkeepers or bar owners, interspersed with moments of lucidity when I saw clearly what a situation or a person really meant, how I'd got it wrong, how I could make amends.

As our interactions with people of all backgrounds and cultures steadily multiply, and as these encounters become less and less predictable, we often lack the distance to stand back and see ourselves from the outside, as someone from another culture might see us.

Should you have behaved in exactly the same way in a business meeting in Kuala Lumpur as you did in San Francisco? Why did that group of Singaporean investors flinch when you made your sales pitch and asked those direct questions in London? Why do members of your multicultural team from Britain and France apparently not get on very well—and yet your colleagues from India seem to communicate so easily with those from China?

It is often worthwhile to write down your feelings about such situations in your journal, so that later you can come back and review your strategy and behaviour—possibly with more positive results on the next occasion.

Nobody has much time these days for standing back and taking a deep breath. But it's amazing how much value can be gained from just reflecting a moment on what you're thinking, feeling, or observing in a new culture or in a new multicultural situation. Self-awareness is one of the most essential qualities of Bamboo Leaders, and yet very few management courses or books emphasize this essential quality.

When I was researching my American novel, I chose to travel in a Greyhound bus across the United States from Albuquerque to the West Coast, stopping at Phoenix, the Grand Canyon, Las Vegas, and finally Los Angeles. If I had any thoughts that my multicultural neighborhood in the Lower East Side of Manhattan was somehow exceptional, I was rudely awakened by that bus journey across the States.

Thank goodness I had my diary with me. Without that, I would not have been able to make sense of the sheer diversity of people I met and made friends with. I recently heard an African-American actress at the Academy Awards nominations declare that, despite the fear-mongers, and demagogues, and anti-immigration lobbyists, despite the enormous amount of work needed for Hollywood to reflect the true reality of American society, 'America is still the superpower of diversity'.

That certainly seemed to be true on that Greyhound journey. Every day I met Mexican Americans, Puerto Ricans, Native Americans, Arab Americans, Hispanics, African Americans, Japanese Americans, Chinese Americans, Indian

Americans, and Korean Americans. When we stopped in the evening at our anonymous motels, I struggled to put down all my encounters of the day and to keep them in some sort of order. But the curious thing was that the more I wrote in my simple scrawl, the more sense I seemed to make not only of that day's impressions but also of the entire experience of America on the road.

Rather than bashing down everything with a typewriter (no laptops in those days!), keeping a diary allowed me to pause and reflect. I was able to gather the thought and inch towards an understanding of it, why I had behaved well or not so well in the situation, what it told me about myself or about other people—and above all, what we might have in common.

I went back to those journals again and again while I was writing *Alphabet City*. Reading them was both therapy and inspiration. It was as if, in the very act of writing, I had paused and waited for the thought, and paused again, and this patience was evident on the page.

Perhaps I also caught glimpses of myself from the outside in the minds of those Chicanos, and Mexicans, and Native Americans. Journaling was a way to write out my loneliness and my fears. I was travelling by myself on a night bus in an unknown country, and sometimes one or the other of the passengers used the restroom. In my diary I wrote, 'Why do they keep going to the back of the bus? Are they drinking alcohol in there or doing drugs? They seem to spend more time in there than in their seat.'

Diaries can be used to register all sorts of confusion and dilemmas. They can also be fertile ground for cross-cultural projects or assignments when you need to talk with someone you trust.

When I was preparing speeches for the CEO and Chairman of that international bank, or working with American and European multinationals, I often went back to my journals on particular countries. I usually found some story or local tradition or interesting linguistic expression in the notes I made on my travels. I included these in the speech I wrote or the cross-cultural workshop I gave, both to enliven it and give the audience the feeling that I knew about them, about their dreams and their beliefs, and that I was addressing them as an equal and a local.

It almost always worked, sometimes in surprising ways. Many business books quote the Chinese expression *wei-ji* for the concept of 'change' as being made up of two Chinese separate characters *wei* and *ji*. Mandarin Chinese characters are not letters of the alphabet but are calligraphic expressions of philosophical or spiritual world-views—in this case *wei* meaning crisis and *ji* meaning opportunity.

This information would have gone down poorly in a speech given by our CEO to an audience in China. The revelation that 'change' could mean both crisis and opportunity would not have come as much of a surprise to a country that endured Mao's Great Leap Forward. A Caucasian could not lecture a civilization with four thousand years of history on the meaning of change.

However, a European country that was undergoing radical readjustments due to the problems of some of the poorer members of the European Union might well look on the Chinese double meaning of *wei* and *ji* as an insight into its current situation. So too might an audience in New York or Chicago when hearing a speech about the Trans-Pacific Partnership Agreement or about the slowdown in the global commodities markets.

My diary and my habit of taking notes in different countries and cultures remain a very useful source of cross-cultural inspiration for me when preparing international speeches, presentations, and training for different countries. If a speech or seminar is to be given in Sao Paolo or Paris, Davos or Bangkok, Tokyo or Vancouver, I have to be ready with a story or background information, a local metaphor, an allusion to that country's music or literature, anything that suggests deeper thought and connection with that audience. It can't just be a cookie-cutter speech for all occasions. Every presentation has to be customized. Every reference has to be local. That's what it means to have a CQ strategy.

HOLD THAT THOUGHT

There is one other mental habit that has helped me greatly in my cross-cultural work—and I am sure it will help you too. You may even be doing it already.

And that is finding a place and a time to focus.

I don't expect many people will tell you this, but cross-cultural work is a vocation. I don't mean that you have to enter holy orders to carry it off successfully. I don't mean that Bamboo Leaders are a select tribe of devotees like Trappist monks. I simply mean that someone who is truly Bamboo Strong has to approach the challenges of the new global economy with a commitment to achieving success— whether that is with diverse workforces, in new and unfamiliar markets, or simply by responding to the tectonic shifts in the global competitive landscape.

All around us is chaos, disruption, innovation, super-connectivity, 24/7 communication (can there be 36/7 communication?), more risk, more unpredictability, more diversity. How can you find time in this multicultural whirlwind for focus? This question needs an answer because the result of all this hyperactivity is that we are often *not present* when crucial signs and signals are being transmitted. These signs are coming to us through body language or through verbal communication while we think we are taking them in. The reality is that we are often travelling on automatic, listening but not translating, seeing but not absorbing. We multitask on our devices and smart phones, and take calls, and shoot off emails, all without actually being there. This is even more the case when it comes to difficult cross-cultural encounters.

We nod and agree or smile and disagree without understanding what the other person, perhaps from another culture or racial, or religious, or ethnic background, is telling us. We are stranded on the island of People Like Us and don't have the energy to get off.

However, what the culturally diverse situation really requires from us is our presence. You don't have to have ADHD to be among the majority of participants in cross-cultural situations who lack the ability to truly focus. This is a pity because such encounters demand more attention from us, more seeing, and more instinctive listening—listening with the whole body—than the people we usually meet on a daily basis.

One of the habits I took up while travelling and working in different countries—and I still observe when I am overseas or in my own country—is visiting a temple, mosque, or church. In my case, this is usually a Buddhist temple. I fell into this habit while travelling in different countries throughout Asia, the Americas, and Europe, and somehow it has never left me.

Whenever I arrive in a new city, I go to search out the nearest Buddhist temple, or if I am in a Muslim country I go to the mosque, or if there is only a Christian church available I go to that. I don't know if I am a particularly spiritual person. I attended many Christian services when I was younger, both as a choirboy at my local church and at my Cambridge college as a member of the chapel choir. But perhaps my church attendance at that time was more an emotional attachment than a spiritual one: I loved the music, the sheer poetry of parts of the Bible, the candles at Christmas, the robes and ceremonies, and the friendships with members of the community.

I found all this in Italy too, although I was never really drawn to Roman Catholicism or its severe strictures and confessionals. I'm not much of a Heaven and Hell person. However, the more I discovered about the strong element of spiritualism or mysticism in people's daily existence in many Asian countries, the more I was drawn to Buddhism. There is something very down-to-earth about Buddhism with its Middle Way and its practices to lead a better and more compassionate life. It is a philosophy, a way to behave and think, rather than a religion with an omniscient god, and avenging angels, and prophets. Above all, it places meditation and mindfulness at its core, and freedom from desires and the noise of ambition.

So whenever I arrive in a new location I seek out the temple. Often this seeking out has led me to the most beautiful, hidden places on mountainsides or the edges of lakes, or to surprising oases of calm and nature like the

Kyomizudera temple in Kyoto, the ancient capital of Japan, or Wat Arun, the Temple of the Golden Dawn, on the banks of the Chao Praya River in Bangkok.

I love slipping my shoes off at the steps to the temple's main hall, with the golden face of Buddha shining between the pillars, and merging into the crowd of celebrants kneeling before the altars piled high with offerings of fruits and sweetmeats. I like the soothing sound of the *moktak*, the wooden clapper being beaten by a stick, the occasional chime of the prayer bell. Above all, I like the murmur of the head priest chanting the sutras, the Buddhist scriptures.

Immediately the noise of the traffic around the compound is blocked out—and the busyness of the day, the effort of getting there, all the worries and plans—and I am within the moment. I feel my whole body becoming intent on just the sound and the chanting. When I attended the Vipassana Buddhist Meditation Centre for foreigners in Yangon, Burma, I remember that it was this intentness, focusing only on the moment without my thoughts wandering, that was the most difficult to achieve. (Vipassana means 'to see things as they really are'.) I was lucky as a foreigner. Unlike the young acolytes who came to the temple to learn meditation and practice to become monks, the instructor did not beat me on my upper shoulders with a rattan stick when my mind wandered or I couldn't maintain my posture.

With the different schools of yoga now sweeping Western countries and becoming such a regular part of fitness programs, it is easy to forget that meditation or mindfulness is essentially a mental training. It helps you to focus on the present, to notice the details of what you see, and to calm your inner turbulence. This in turn carries you into higher levels of consciousness.

Those who relate and work across cultures need this higher consciousness, both for the bigger picture it affords as well as the observation of tiny details you might otherwise miss.

Try this little experiment. Take a look at your smart phone or device. Just look at it for moment and write down how you would describe it to someone who doesn't know what it looks like: black screen, white button at bottom, thin metal case, little sliding rectangles of buttons on the side, titanium coating, pin-sized hole at top left corner, short vertical line, larger round circle of glass at top left corner on back, and so on.

When you've written down your list, press the circle button at the bottom of the front casing—or wherever the screen turns on—and see the whole thing light up. Now imagine you have to explain all the things that your phone does: it writes and sends emails, it connects you to the worldwide Web, it guides you when you are lost walking or driving, it talks to you (perhaps even in foreign languages), it plays your favorite music, it shows videos, it shows you people who like you or your work, it connects you to anyone you choose anywhere in the world.

In other words, the phone has become a sort of second you. It has become a metaphor of you.

When we focus on the present and perhaps on one small object in front of us, the mind may seem to shrink, but in fact it expands. It brings new meaning to life. It voyages on the imagination. It lights up with greater and higher energies.

If we just stop and see, if we train our mind towards mindfulness, we will notice the subtle nuances and hints of multicultural encounters. You don't have to be religious or even spiritual to be mindful. You just have to focus. That's why I always go to some place on my speaking tours, or on my training and mentoring assignments, where I can hear the sound of the *moktak*—or its mental equivalent.

TRIED AND TESTED

While we're on the subject of mental preparation, another helpful way to approach cross-cultural encounters—one also related to mindfulness—is to create a system and write it down.

My friend and mentor John Eggen, the American publishing and marketing guru, often quotes the books of management luminary, W. Edwards Deming, who is best known for his work in Japan after the Second World War. Dr. Deming helped Japanese leaders of industry rebuild the country from ground zero. In his famous System of Profound Knowledge, which was credited with guiding Japan out of its crisis, he revealed that 94 percent of all failures come from lack of a time-tested system. 'When you use a time-tested system, especially a written plan,' said Dr. Deming, 'you greatly increase your chances of success.'

Of course, your plan also needs to be subject to revision. John Eggen quotes the example of NASA, which has a history of landing vehicles on the moon with amazing accuracy. The moon is 240 thousand miles away from earth. In order to land their rockets, NASA engineers always start with an extensive written plan. However, from the time they launch their rocket until the moment the vehicle lands on the moon, NASA engineers are revising 99 percent of the plan as unforeseen circumstances arise.

Obstacles appear, equipment malfunctions, perhaps the rocket encounters asteroids in space. I recently watched the expedition of Major Tim Peake, the first British astronaut to walk in space, with rapt attention—especially when he arrived at the space station and the module would not at first dock correctly. Later in the expedition, his first walk in space was curtailed by another malfunction within the spacesuit's air-filtering system.

The circumstances may change, but the necessity does not. It's always best to have a written plan in place, and this usually consists of a number of lists with items to be checked off. I use a similar kind of list when I go to a new speaking venue. I have my pre-speaking packing list: clickers in two sizes, batteries, props, introduction message, speech cards, back-up USB with slides, extension cables, adapters from one voltage or socket type to another, monitor adapter, rubber bands, back-up speech cards (you might drop or lose a set), books, audience questionnaires, speaker biography, book stands, signing fountain pen, and so on.

I have a similar post-event list and follow-up list of things to do.

A speaking engagement for an international audience requires a lot of adaptation and preparation, rather like working across cultures or with new multicultural teams. I may need a welcome and sign-off slide with words in another language. I may need a translator. I will certainly have to check my references and what I may think is amusing or good fun to perform against the cultural norms and expectations of my audience. And I need a back-up plan when something goes wrong (as it always does).

It is no different with cross-cultural assignments. You need to prepare a number of checklists that you can sign off on each time you encounter a new challenge—whether it's a meeting with international business clients from Argentina or Indonesia; or holding a virtual leadership strategy meeting with teams from your New York, Sydney, Wellington, ASEAN, and China offices; or attending a charity raising brainstorming with inputs from colleagues of many racial, ethnic, and religious backgrounds.

Such meetings can be stressful if you don't come prepared. It is tempting to attempt to wing it every time we do anything cross-cultural. After all, people are supposed to be the same everywhere—surely allowances will be made. But usually we end up being disoriented, flustered, and disappointed if we can't achieve the desired results.

That's where the tried-and-tested system comes into play. Your company could perhaps save millions of dollars if you have a well-prepared list of the essential points to cover, the best way to approach them in this cross-cultural context, the kind of mistakes and blunders to avoid, and many other potential challenges.

CRISIS IS OPPORTUNITY

However, the best-laid plans of mice and men can go astray. Sometimes what is right in front of you changes even as you are looking at it. When this happens, don't forget the lesson of NASA landing its rockets on the moon: revising a list is just as important as making one.

One of my objectives while I was in Mandalay in Upper Burma in the 1990s was to discover some towns that were off the beaten track but that would reveal something about the British colonial period in Burma. Mandalay was very interesting. However, it was also well documented and visited, and after a few weeks I thought I knew it pretty thoroughly.

This was mostly due to my circle of friends at the Mandalay Puppet Theatre and our clandestine bicycle trips to outlying villages and towns. What I really wanted was to go further, to somewhere completely unknown, where *The temple-bells are callin', an' it's there that I would be, By the old Moulmein Pagoda, looking lazy at the sea.* The Kipling poem was still in my head.

So together with my Mandalay friends, I hatched a plan. My guide, Ne Win, and my driver, Min, would accompany me by car to the old British garrison town of Shwebo, which was about 110 kilometers northwest of Mandalay. There we would stay in a government rest house, which would mean being registered as official visitors. How would we achieve this, considering foreigners were not allowed to travel out of Mandalay?

I had a pre-existing plan. The letter from the ministry of tourism in Yangon, which had been signed by the minister of tourism, allowed me to travel to certain destinations as a travel writer for international magazines. Shwebo was on the list of places I had applied to visit when I first made my visa application to the Burmese consulate in Hong Kong.

However, this name had been omitted from the official passe-partout I was issued at the ministry of tourism in Yangon. So I had persuaded the general in charge to include the sentence 'Permission to enter places of interest to foreign tourists' at the bottom of the list of allowed locations. That was the plan. As an extension to the plan, I would lie flat on the back seat of the car when we passed military checkpoints on the way to Shwebo. If the checkpoint guards spotted me, Min or Ne Win would hand over the ministry's letter expressly authorizing me to enter places of interest to foreign tourists.

At the first checkpoint, the soldiers read the letter through at least ten times, made several phone calls, and asked why I was lying down on the back seat. There was a lot of discussion about this, and for a while it seemed like we would be turned back or worse. However, the soldiers finally relented and let us through. Once we were back on the highway, I revised the plan in my head.

At the next checkpoint, I sat up in plain view and appeared as confident as possible. The soldiers looked me over with a frown, read the letter a couple of times, and this time just shrugged. However, before they allowed us to pass, they asked why I was dressed in Burmese attire of *longyi*, Mandarin shirt, and short Burmese tunic jacket. Ne Win explained that I found Burmese attire much more comfortable in the heat and wanted to take photographs of myself in front of Burmese tourist attractions for the readers of my articles.

The soldiers still seemed puzzled. However, Ne Win had been a prize debater at Mandalay University (before the military government closed it down), and his eloquence seemed to win them over. Once more, we were allowed to pass.

Finally, we entered the dusty, old town of Shwebo, with its myriad pagodas and crumbling colonial-style arcades, coming to a halt in front of the government rest house. The old Burmese clerk at the check-in counter had clearly never seen an Englishman before, although I could see there were Chinese and possibly Japanese guests in the lounge. He asked for my passport, and then read the letter that Ne Win presented to him.

'Why?' he said with a frown, and I saw him surreptitiously slide my passport into his desk drawer. 'Why is he here? Shwebo is not on this list.'

'He is allowed to go to tourist destinations,' said Ne Win. 'It says so at the bottom of the letter.'

The old desk clerk growled, folded the letter, and reached for a key on the wall behind him. 'I'll give him a room for now, but not for you two. You must find another place.'

Clearly, the old man wanted to separate us. Taking the key, I told the others to wait for me in the lobby and hurried up to my room. However, just as I reached the corner of the first flight of stairs, I looked back and saw the old clerk stretch for the telephone on his desk.

I revised my plan as soon as I got through the door and closed it behind me. Removing my *longyi*, Mandarin shirt, and jacket, I took my trousers, T-shirt, and shoes out of my shoulder bag and put them on. Burmese attire may have been comfortable, but it certainly wasn't worth being mistaken for 007.

Just then I heard a loud noise on the street, the bang of lorry doors, and the sound of boots on metal. I looked out the window, and to my horror saw a number of army lorries blocking the street. They were filled with armed soldiers.

Why had I not included this possibility in my plan? I was taking a huge risk in what was in effect occupied Burma. In my quest for historical colour and perhaps adventure, I had put two loyal Burmese friends in danger, and I was going to need all my resources to get them out of it.

Returning to the lobby, I found Ne Win and Min sitting rather shamefacedly with two Burmese officials dressed in black jackets, and with name badges in black and white pinned to them. They were looking through my letter, my passport (from end to end and back again), and the papers belonging to Ne Win and Min. It was time to once more revise my plan.

I took out an American Express magazine from my bag and revealed a big photographic spread in the middle with one of my articles on the city of Chiang Rai in Thailand. I pointed out my name at the top of the article, and the colorful pagodas and temples. Delving into my scant knowledge of Shwebo's history, I also mentioned that I was interested in writing about King Alaungpaya, ruler of Burma in the mid-eighteenth century.

Somehow it worked. The officials talked among themselves for a while, and then told me that Shwebo was no longer a forgotten town in Burmese history. It was the headquarters of the Sagaing region military command. I immediately sat up straighter and apologized on behalf of us all for straying into such an off-limits area.

There was an awkward silence. The officials still seemed to be hesitating. Then I remembered something in our prepared plan. I looked hard at Ne Win, who produced something from his shirt pocket and slid it across the table: an envelope containing two fifty US dollar bills.

Within minutes we were on our way back to Mandalay, the passport and letter safely in my hands.

I'm not telling this story to recommend small, brown envelopes, except in a real crisis. However, I am recommending you revise your plans always in light of circumstances—and still try to reach your objectives.

I escaped from Shwebo with the knowledge that this was the current military command center for the Sagaing region. If I had been a British spy, my goal would have been reached through numerous revisions of my plan. As it was, I did discover a new Burmese destination off the beaten track with lots of local colour, even though it would be several more years before tourists would be allowed to go there.

Multicultural situations often develop rapidly without you having any control of how or where they are going. Sometimes you can mistake a smile for an invitation to enter when it's a smile of embarrassment, or you can read silence to mean assent when it signifies the opposite.

If you're like me, you can easily find yourself thinking the wrong thing when there's a perfectly innocent explanation. For example, I was recently convinced that my taxi driver in Taiwan was deliberately taking me the long way around to the Kuomintang museum in Taipei because he was hoping for a higher fare. In fact, all he really wanted to do was to chat to me in English about the Japanese-style *enka* (folk ballads) he was playing on his taxi CD player. I remember how idiotic I felt when I worked this one out.

If the cross-cultural rocket is to hit your moon, you will need to constantly revise your plans. You will need to check your anger or frustration, breathe deeply and reconsider. Most of the time, it's because of a misunderstanding or a misreading of a situation. Sometimes it's just an experience you have to name and file away for future reference—or preferably write down. Ask a colleague about it. Better still ask a sympathetic person from that culture or a cross-cultural mentor like myself to explain it to you. The situation often turns out to be completely different to what you imagine.

This constant readjustment is how the brain works and is the way a true Bamboo Leader develops an effective CQ Strategy.

THE ANSWER LIES IN THE QUESTION

The fact is I was constantly asking questions as I revised my plan for visiting Shwebo or indeed for handling the Taipei taxi driver.

What would be a better way to merge into the background and not become an object of suspicion when passing through checkpoints?

What should I do when my idea of looking Burmese didn't work?

Why should I rely on an official letter from a distant capital city in a land of lawless provinces ruled by military overlords?

What was my fail-safe plan?

What would I do to protect my local friends or not put them in awkward situations?

Why was the desk clerk attempting to separate us? How much could I rely on local friends like Ne Win or Min? Was Burmese friendliness superficial or real?

Did they really support my plan to go to Shwebo?

Why was the Taipei taxi driver talking to me so loudly about Taiwanese ballads?

Was he simply pleased to be practicing English? If so, why had he turned off his meter?

And so on.

Of course, you can't enter every cross-cultural situation and ask these questions out loud. If I asked the Taipei taxi driver why he was talking so much and driving with such nonchalance, I might have offended him. Instead, I asked him about the Japanese-Taiwanese ballads, compared them to what I had heard in Tokyo, and discovered he was a genuine aficionado.

You may be in a meeting with clients, or customers, or partners from another country, or from another team in your own company, and find the discussion they propose very strange. You may be disturbed by the way they are silent on certain points, or the fact that they defer to the eldest in the room but never ask you to speak. Or you may be perplexed that they simply seem to want a download of the bullet points on your slides and don't want to hear a presentation at all. In all these situations and many similar ones, ask yourself *why*.

Or rather, sit back and reframe why into an indirect question as a way of finding out more. My question to the Taipei taxi driver was in fact a way of sounding him out— making sure he wasn't going to abduct me! Your question at the meeting where they don't seem to want a presentation could be 'Would you like a proposal with all the points included in bullet form?' or 'How do you usually obtain the information you require?'

While you wait and listen for the answer, don't look angry. The answer may come elliptically. It may not be what you want to hear. It may be that you notice signals being exchanged with someone outside the room. It may be that the other party seems to be waiting for something or someone before taking action. When this person or 'something' becomes manifest, you may kick yourself for not seeing the situation earlier. If you dig deeper, ask more questions and show patience. An answer always comes.

Advanced CQ Strategy is all about waiting for answers. It's also about testing your conclusions, your discoveries, and what you know already of this culture (CQ Knowledge) to see if it all adds up. True Bamboo Leaders will not consider action until their observations, hypotheses, and plans are tested for accuracy.

I was recently in Bali talking with Arief, an Indonesian executive. Arief was interested in my participation in an exporting programme for the Indonesian government based on my cultural intelligence programs and workshops.

From what I knew of Indonesia, the way business is done in that country is rather circuitous and laid back. Relationships are much more important than rushing into contracts. Negotiations are carried out slowly and with reference to many other factors such as evidence of long-term commitment. The Bahasa Indonesian language has twelve different ways of saying no (and several ways of saying yes when no is meant). Above all, I knew about the Indonesian expression *jam karet*, meaning 'rubber time', which was coined in reference to the long lunches, relaxed dinners, and less than punctual approach to doing business in the archipelago.

So when I went to my first meeting with Arief, I fully expected him to be late. In fact, I was so confident of this— having experienced just such an encounter with an Indonesian businessman a few days before—that I took a longer swim than usual in the hotel swimming pool.

Imagine my surprise, therefore, when I arrived in the restaurant to find Arief already sitting there, with his MacBook Pro laptop at his dining place, a speakerphone and mic in his ears, talking loudly to someone on the other end. I rather sheepishly sat down and waited for Arief to finish his call. 'Sorry I'm late. I wasn't sure if you meant twelve noon sharp or rather lunchtime.' Arief smiled and closed his laptop. 'I think you've been picking up some Indonesian habits. We are not all on *jam karet*,' he said or words to that effect.

He was right. In all my dealings with Arief, I found him to be extremely precise and on the ball. It's true that, when it came to contracts, he tended to be a little more vague, as if waiting for further evidence of our relationship before committing anything to paper. However, I never felt I was being misled or that the business itself was not going to happen.

He introduced me to key people at the government agencies; he took over most of the high-level negotiations with government ministers; he attended a business and investment convention in Jakarta on my behalf, and he organized visits to the country's special economic zones. He phoned me regularly to keep me up to date—and he always called on time.

I therefore read the cues and adjusted my plan accordingly. I stopped thinking of all Indonesians as having the *jam karet* attitude to business, and I prepared myself to negotiate with very precise and intelligent executives from both the government and the private sector. I was therefore able to develop and deliver a successful cultural intelligence programme for Indonesian exporters on time and on budget.

There were other occasions when I didn't pick up on the cultural clues in front of me and revise my plan—and I paid the price. This was usually because I didn't test what I thought I knew, or what experts had told me about a particular culture, against my own experience.

You have to find more than one source on a culture, someone who can confirm or negate your observations. As discussed in Part 3, one of the best ways to test for accuracy is to use a cultural coach or mentor, someone who knows the culture you're interpreting in depth as well as your own cultural background. It's also worthwhile to ask for advice or guidance from a local person or even from the person with whom you are dealing. Arief was an excellent guide for me: he showed me what my behaviour implied about Indonesian business and quickly made it clear that it wasn't all like that.

CQ Strategy is all about testing hypotheses for a new cultural or multicultural situation. The best way to measure your observations is to acquire CQ Knowledge, seek out the views of as many informed people as possible, and revise your plan in the light of the questions you ask and the replies you receive.

ANTICIPATE, ANTICIPATE, ANTICIPATE

Ultimately the success of your strategy relies on managing your expectations. If Arief had not set me right, I would have held the wrong—or least wrong in some cases—expectations for Indonesian business.

Quite often our expectations of a new culture are hopelessly optimistic, stereotypical, or overly pessimistic. And yet we often march into new markets in another country, or into a new work culture, or even into marriage to someone with a different ethnic, national, or religious background to ours without managing our expectations.

When I went to live in Japan, I had perhaps unrealistic expectations of the way Japanese people would reach out to me, a foreigner. I was hoping to forge a close relationship with another Japanese. It didn't happen, and the longer it didn't happen, the more I lowered my expectations to the point where the culture seemed manageable. I could get by on politeness and occasional kindness, on relationships with expatriate friends, and on my plans to write about some of the unknown corners of this fascinating country. I knew that I was likely to remain an outsider in Japan, and I used this position to observe its society and culture. In short, I used my CQ Strategy.

In Hong Kong, it was different. Here I expected a more colonial, rather British culture that was more international than Japan and more welcoming to foreigners. To a certain extent I was right. However, my expectations were entirely wrong in regard to how authentically Chinese the territory had remained. The key to that discovery was becoming part of a Hong Kong Chinese family.

And yet, perhaps my time in Japan helped me to adjust relatively smoothly to Simon's family's life. I knew when to flex and when not to flex, when to take off my shoes at the outer lintel and when not, when to keep silent, and when to assert myself. Above all I knew how to use my expectations to imagine what life would be like in such a tight space with relatives whose language I barely understood. When you change your expectations, it's amazing what you can achieve.

If you are about to enter a new cross-cultural situation, ask yourself what you expect to happen. What are you hoping to gain? What are your biggest fears and your biggest hopes? What do you intend to learn? How many of your own judgments or preconceptions will you have to suspend or modify (thousand-year-old eggs are delicious in rice congee, for example, contrary to my initial expectations)? It should be part of your CQ Strategy to write all these thoughts down in your plan and to discuss them with others.

Many business leaders go into new cross-cultural ventures with excellent goals but absurdly high expectations. They fail to take into account the importance of personal relationships, and of developing these over a long period of time, as a measure of trust and commitment. The narrow emphasis on bottom-line goals is often reflected in disproportionate expectations of how responsive the other party will be to their approach.

If such business leaders are wise, they will lower their expectations in response to the challenges. This is where the example of NASA's engineers comes in again. Rockets do not land on the moon without carefully written, tried-and-tested systems that are then constantly revised. This does not mean that you should lose your expectations—they are vital for your motivation—but you have to manage them to come out ahead.

Are you really going to sign a contract on that three-day business trip to Beijing? Will that contract be final, or it will it be subject to revision? Are you really going to learn to speak fluent German after a five-day course in Munich, or are you going to know enough to get around by taxi, catch a train, or greet your German clients at the beginning of a video conference? There may be a positive outcome to this. For example, even if you are not fluent in German, you may be asked to be the company's lead host when important German investors are invited to a festive dinner in your home city of Toronto, Guangzhou, Osaka, or Los Angeles.

Accurately anticipating outcomes almost always means modifying your expectations, which in turn can lead to a positive result. Bamboo Leaders have to be ready for such changes. Spending time with people from other cultures gives them the necessary experience to adapt to each cross-cultural situation as it unfolds.

If they spend their time exclusively with an expatriate circle that keeps local people at arms length, it is much more difficult to achieve this. We all know the feeling. We are at a social gathering with guests from another culture, and we don't really feel confortable. We assume there's a big distance that we can only bridge by smiling a lot. It happens quite often. Sometimes we're sitting in a seminar or workshop with people from different countries and despite our best intentions, we still feel a bit awkward.

It even happens at international events with people from the same industry. I was recently speaking at an annual conference of international accountancy firms in Hong Kong, and it was noticeable that people from similar parts of the globe, such as the Chinese, Singaporeans, Japanese, and Malaysians, kept together. Those from Australia, Britain, and the Americas formed another group, while those from Turkey, Slovenia, Hungary, France, Germany, and Holland formed yet another. It wasn't quite as rigid as that, but it was moving that way. My subject was cultural intelligence, so you would think that everyone communicated well across borders and continents. Well, think again.

The problem is that we fall back on safety, often because we have not made the effort to plan social interactions with other cultures and imagine how they might be. If those attendees had developed the CQ Strategy I revealed to them, they might have been more able to reach out socially across their cultural groupings. CQ Strategy asks us to anticipate, to think ahead, to have a plan. If it's a drink with new prospects from Hungary and Slovenia, you have to imagine what might be good topics of conversation, what is in the news, what business issues might hit the twin targets of empathy and solidarity.

Your topics may fall flat. However, the effort to prepare them will strengthen your CQ Strategy and further your cross-cultural effectiveness. Next time you will be more ready to deal with the ideas and suggestions of members of your international teams, or perhaps of those colleagues in your own office who come from many different racial, national, and religious backgrounds.

You will have experience not only of developing your CQ Drive and CQ Knowledge. You will also know how to use them to land your rocket on the moon.

To create your own Cultural Intelligence (CQ) Planner, with action points and strategies from this chapter, please visit www.davidcliveprice.com/planner

PERFORMANCE

CQ ACTION

STEPPING ONTO THE STAGE

So here's a trick I learned about cross-cultural encounters.

Imagine you are stepping out onto a stage. If you are an extrovert or have a natural taste for the dramatic, imagine in addition that the cameras are rolling.

Every little gesture you make, all your facial expressions—including having little or no expression at all—and all your words, your tone of voice, and your inflections, are aimed at giving a good performance. You want to appear as someone who is clearly understood in this situation and who is accepted, even trusted, as having the basic good manners any respected person would possess in this culture.

Performance, or CQ Action, is what will get you there.

CQ Action is the most expressive of the four capabilities that support the development of your cultural intelligence. It draws on your CQ Knowledge and CQ Strategy to show you when, where, and how you should use your social skills. Some of this is very basic and nonverbal, such as knowing when to take your shoes off before entering a temple or mosque, when women should cover their head in Muslim countries, how to exchange business cards politely and professionally in Asia, how to offer or acknowledge a toast at a banquet in China, and so on. These kinds of interaction are usually gathered together under the heading of social and business etiquette in how-to business guides and are very useful to know.

However, as a busy executive or business leader, you can't be expected to learn every culture's norms of etiquette. Sometimes the effort to do so is overwhelming. It makes self-conscious participants commit more mistakes than they normally would by simply watching and observing.

I once met Bob, a high-level coaching client, in the lobby of a five-star hotel in Bangkok. He had just flown in from a business meeting in Tokyo and had arrived slightly flustered in the heat, a few minutes late for our meeting. Apologizing to me for the delay, Bob headed for the check-in counter where he could see a welcoming party waiting for him— the general manager and a perfectly made-up Thai woman, dressed in gold and lilac silks, and holding a garland of orchids in her hand.

Bob had only just begun doing business in Asia on behalf of an American multinational, and he was clearly anxious to do things correctly. So as he approached the welcoming party at the desk, he took out his little silver box of business cards and readied two cards in his hand to exchange in the customary way. He was a tall man, which made it slightly awkward for him to bend forward at the check-in desk to receive the garland of orchids around his neck.

He had clearly been studying Thai etiquette on the plane, or perhaps had picked it up (Performance again) from the air stewardesses at the airport. In any case, as he bent forward for the garland, he also raised his two hands in tented formation at his forehead in the Thai Buddhist greeting called the *pranom*. He also attempted to say '*Sawasdee Ka*' ('Hello'), and for some reason—perhaps because he had just been in Tokyo—he converted his incline of the head to receive the orchids into a Japanese-style low bow.

The result was that he keeled over right there on the marble floor of the hotel, with his business cards and silver case flying in all directions. Bellboys and receptionists rushed to pick him up.

Fortunately Bob was a good-tempered guy, and he saw the funny side. Order was soon restored, and I helped him towards the bar for a consolatory drink. But, as he said ruefully over his first Mai Thai cocktail, 'I've got to take one step at a time with all this etiquette business.'

'Well, at least you tried,' I said. 'Some people never make the effort. And did you see the reaction of the Thais in the lobby?'

'Yeah, that surprised me,' said Bob. 'They were laughing, but they didn't seem to be laughing at me.'

Bob had seen what often seems to happen when foreigners make blunders of etiquette and behaviour in other cultures. They are appreciated for it. The mere act of trying to fit in or do the right thing gives you brownie points. The incident in the lobby resulted in outstanding service and many more charming Thai smiles for our business dinner that evening, and Bob told me that for the rest of his stay in Bangkok he was treated like a king.

Bob was what you might call a clue reader. We are not all readers of clues. Many of us walk blindly through new cross-cultural situations barely noticing any differences. If we do, we often consider them too 'foreign', too bizarre, or too much of an embarrassing effort to try and imitate them. But like all actors who are worth their reviews, the ones who really succeed in cross-cultural work not only notice little gestures and customs, they actively reproduce them. They get into character.

How people greet each other is an inevitable first step. I've actually practiced the different levels of bows in Asia in front of a mirror: a slight incline of the head in China when shaking hands, a forty-five-degree bow in South Korea to someone senior or elder or simply to show respect; a ninety-degree bow (and various gradations according to status and seniority) in Japan. However, I would not have dreamed of using these without spending some time in each country and watching how they are performed.

Much depends on your experience or how long you intend to spend in the culture. I lived in my little Italian hilltop town for so long, I learned the importance of the *ora di riposo* after lunch in order to awake refreshed for evening business and pre-dinner activity, including the Italian habit of *la passeggiata*—walking around town in your best clothes to meet and greet friends and business acquaintances. It was a performance, an opportunity to *far la bella figura* (make an elegant impression), and it was communal at the same time.

There are social habits and community skills like these to pick up in every culture, and you can quickly learn the lines that should accompany them. In Mediterranean, Asian, African, and Latin American cultures, it is usually very acceptable to ask about families and friends and where people come from. Even in business situations and at dinners, it is often a good idea to talk about your family, children, education, and marriages rather than business itself.

However, in northern European or American business circles, it would be considered strange if you asked about wives and children rather than about business. I would also not recommend talking about politics in China or Hong Kong, or even in Singapore, although it would be acceptable in Taiwan. Unless you know someone well in America or Britain, you would probably keep off topics like elections, migration, religious beliefs, or independence movements. It all depends on the context. I've had some very illuminating discussions on English Premier League football in China, and on rugby in Japan, and, of course, on cricket in Australia, New Zealand, Sri Lanka, India, and Pakistan. I've even been initiated into the mysteries of ice hockey in Canada. Usually there is some recent topic that you can introduce into cross-cultural conversations to build rapport with your counterparts, whether it's the latest economic developments that affect this country, sport or fashion, music or theatre. You just have to show that you have a global mindset and are aware at the same time of local concerns and culture.

In other words, you need to build up your range of social skills so that you can perform well across cultures. It all starts with picking up those initial clues, learning your lines, and trying things out.

TREADING THE BOARDS

One of the ways I learned how to get along and be accepted by my Chinese family was to learn the sounds of certain Cantonese expressions that came up time and again in our daily life in my One Room in Kowloon.

This was quite hard to do because as soon as I got the hang of *gay ho ma*? (how are you?), or *ho mafaan* (very difficult), or *ho sek* (delicious), and strung them together with a few other phrases, I would get the tones wrong. Either that, or something about the way I delivered the phrases, meant that my Chinese relatives, including the younger children, would stare at me with incomprehension. So I'd have to get Simon or one of his sisters to repeat what I was trying to say in the correct way. I would then imitate it.

In other words, I was acting like a linguistic toddler, which reflected my general inability to behave in the same way as the rest of my family. I had to learn new steps every day as if I were walking for the first time: light incense sticks and say a prayer to the ancestors with three bows of the head before the corner shrine; pass my rice bowl when emptied to a sister at the rice cooker with the words *bun wun m'goy* (half a bowl, please); buy new shoes and clothes to wear on the first day of Lunar New Year; eat vegetarian *jai* over the holidays; and many other traditions and customs.

However, slowly I began to acclimatize myself to these different behaviors, and I began to pronounce those basic Cantonese words so that I was fully understood. It was something to do with getting in character. I don't mean putting on a costume or another persona. I just mean that in order to get the right intonation and be understood, I had to feel like my family members must feel as they made these requests. It was both a mental and an emotional thing. It was as if I had to become a little bit Cantonese myself to say the phrases correctly.

I found the same in Italian, with its full repertoire of extravagant gestures, and I have had a similar experience when speaking Japanese or Korean, French or German. It is impolite to openly mimic people from other cultures. It can seem like mockery or stereotyping, even if it's affectionate (we have an old comedy series on British TV about the British and French wartime resistance called '*Allo 'Allo!* that parodies the way a French barman or his girlfriend might speak English or a British airman might speak French, along with their supposed national attitudes). However, to speak a language with effect, in many ways you have to *become another character*—you have to identify with the feelings of people from other cultures when they use their language.

I have noticed the same occurs when I speak English with people from different backgrounds and cultures, say Swiss German or Filipino, Spanish or Brazilian. Over a period of time living in these cultures, I have shortened or lengthened my vowels, cut off my sentences, made the past tense present, changed plurals to singular, and many other unconscious verbal tricks so that in fact my English sounds like theirs.

You might think this is rather condescending, as if by turning my English into Chinglish or Singlish (Singaporean English) I am putting my interlocutors down. However, I don't see it as my mission to convert the rest of the world to Cambridge English. I do see it as my mission to get on the same wavelength with as many cultures and peoples as possible. Something in my CQ inclines me to flex my language just as much as I flex my behaviour to accompany that language.

When I return to London from North America I have a strange mid-Atlantic twang. When I come back from Asia, I speak an odd English with a slight Chinglish accent that surprises and amuses my friends, colleagues, and relations. And yet I don't know I am doing it.

Perhaps it is because I am a cultural actor, I try to get under the skin of the character I'm portraying. Language or adapting your language is just the first step in identifying with individuals from other cultures and then being able to behave like they do. It's all part of the same mission to build understanding.

Of course, it wouldn't be a good idea to just mimic people and hope for the best. I'm not suggesting you immediately go out and mirror the walks of Chinese, or American, or British tourists, or the way they sound. There are moments to flex, and moments when you shouldn't flex in order to avoid giving offence. I wouldn't use my Chinglish when talking to the master and fellows of my Cambridge college. I assume a different role and language for that.

However, I don't consciously change my behaviour for one or the other context. I do it unconsciously, at the level of my cultural intelligence. This enables me to see the world differently, whether it's the world of a Cambridge college, a small town in the Züri Oberland, a rustic valley in Tuscany, the C-suite floors of an international bank, or a Chinese family apartment in Hong Kong.

We are often performing and presenting ourselves in different ways in front of other people. I was performing a role in that international bank, a role I sometimes switched according to my expatriate or Chinese audience. I needed to be a lateral thinker, decisive, good with deadlines, responsive to the harassed requests of senior executives. Most of these roles were new to me, but I was soon flexing along with the best of them.

Later, when I learned to perform in front of an audience as a keynote speaker and workshop leader, I was surprised to discover that the art of self-presentation emerged from my boyhood acting roles and university college plays. Almost everything we do is a performance of some kind, usually with the intention of leaving a positive impression without false notes, or awkward silences, or garbled lines.

I prepare carefully for these presentations and workshops, training myself with a video camera and rehearsing many times over, so that I will look natural and confident when I speak in front of an audience. It's the same with CQ Action. You have to prepare off stage, pick up the gestures and behaviour that might be appropriate, speak a few words in the local language, and model yourself on the voice and style of a certain local person you know, whether they're from Santiago, Stockholm, or Saigon.

You may have to negotiate or prepare a contract with them tomorrow. Find out how it might feel if you were in their place. Who would you have to know in local government? How do they sound and think? How will they show positive interest or start to build a relationship?

You don't have to be a method actor like Marlon Brando to succeed. But you do need to know how to perform.

LANGUAGE SURVIVAL KIT

In order to get going in my daily interactions with my Chinese family, I started off with short words or phrases in Cantonese. The beauty of short phrases is that you can practice with them and see if they work before you move onto anything more complex.

Results-driven international executives rarely have time to learn more than simple phrases—unless they attend one of their company's intensive language courses, say in Mandarin or Spanish (the two up-and-coming challengers to the global domination of English).

Even then, they often practice with simple sentences while they are learning the language. Research has shown that a modicum of language knowledge can greatly help with social interaction, even if it means simply dropping a word or two of a recently learnt phrase into your English conversation.

When I first went to South Korea, English was not spoken outside Seoul and often not within Seoul—except in hotels and certain business circles. Since I could not read Hangul (the Korean alphabet) or speak Korean, my technique for getting around the country was simple. I would use the following phrases:

- *Annyeonghi-haseyo* (hello)
- *Annyeonghi-kaseyo* (goodbye)
- *ye* (yes)
- *aniyo* (no)
- *chuseyo* (please)
- *kamsa hamnida* (thank you)
- *mian hamnida* (sorry or excuse me)
- *olmayeyo* (how much)
- *odi* (where)

This last word was really useful, because you could join it with the interrogative *–nikka* and combine it with all kinds of useful objects as in *beoseu jeongnyuso* (bus station) *odi ib nikka?* (where is the bus station?).

Brilliant! Those simple phrases combined with 'hotel', or 'restaurant', or 'train' and many other useful necessities took me safely around most of the Korean peninsula, up into the mountains of the East Coast, deep into the temple-dotted valleys of Chirisan, and across to the ancient capitals of the Korean kings.

If simple words can unlock a few thousand years of a country's history, it's definitely worth learning them—and using them. Language is not only an important part of CQ Knowledge that enables you to understand a culture, it is also a central part of CQ Action.

Even in an office situation in another culture, this little technique can be extremely effective. Need to get a report quickly from your company's Spanish economist? Drop a pleasant greeting in Spanish, and a comment on the weather into your English conversation (and a *muchas gracias*, of course). Need to get from one end of the airport to another in a hurry in Beijing? Ask for basic directions in Mandarin, and add *xie xie ni* (thank you) at the end.

One of my other techniques is to listen on a regular basis to what local people are saying, and then work out or ask what they mean. It may be a little local saying or an expression for being tired (*stanco da morire*—an Italian expression meaning 'tired to death'). It may be *Klatschblase* (literally 'gossip bladder' in German) or *fanfarron* ('show-off' in Spanish). As long as they are in regular use and colloquial, such words or phrases are like a little doorway into another culture. They get you accepted. They colour your presentations in front of audiences in other countries. They encourage people to help you.

Next time you go on a business trip to another country, or find yourself posted to another culture, or have to communicate across borders with multicultural teams, make a little list of words or phrases that might be helpful. Usually, you will find that the same phrases are required in almost all languages. Once you have mastered one set, you have the technique to master others.

Languages are expressions of local culture, values, and beliefs. They are also indicators of how much we all have in common. In terms of rapport and understanding, a little language goes a long way.

ADAPT OR DIE

Now you may not want to hear this—it may remind you of someone you know —but I have to say it anyway. Don't do what a friend of mine does whenever he travels.

And that is shout—in both English and the local language.

I don't know why this is exactly, but Michael cannot turn down the volume control in foreign places, or even when talking to people from different backgrounds in his own office building. Instead of becoming subtler and more nuanced in his speech and general manner when he travels, he goes the other way. Everything about him becomes bigger and louder.

It usually starts on the plane with the flight attendants. I have travelled with him on several occasions on airlines from Latin America or the Middle East. Somehow he feels he has to *make himself understood.* He views each interaction as a potential minefield of misunderstanding. He therefore overemphasizes, repeats himself in English or even in a few words of the other language, and generally becomes larger than life.

I don't know if Michael believes communication will become easier like this or that he will have his requests met more quickly. He seems to think that loudness equals authority in another culture—and that, because he's away from home, he has to exert his authority more.

Sometimes I drop a hint that he is perhaps coming over a bit strong. I even mention that in countries such as those of the airlines on which we are flying, loudness signifies the opposite of authority. Leaders adopt a quiet and calm manner in which harmony is preserved. Since face is of paramount importance, every effort is made to maintain the smooth surface of things.

I am sure Michael does not mean to appear overbearing or rude. The problem is that his lack of volume control makes him look like the worst kind of business traveller—the type who arrives in another culture and wants everything to be done just as it is at home, and who backs up a point of view with a very direct, impatient manner and a loud voice.

Of course, there is a difference between reducing the volume and not being heard at all. As I discovered in my Chinese family, if I spoke without a certain amount of emphasis, I would still be misunderstood, or worse, ignored. You have to get inside the language when you are speaking, even when simply mimicking the sound of a phrase.

Imagine that you have a conductor in your head and you are the orchestra. The music you are struggling to express rises and falls. It becomes *accelerato* or *andante* following the cues of the conductor and the written score. When you are speaking in a foreign language, you are looking for those cues, and you're not going to hear them if you are shouting. Equally, you are not going to hear them if your contribution is so *pianissimo* as to be negligible.

Entering other cultures requires us to be assertive—but only up to a point. Like the sections in a musical ensemble, you have to listen and then contribute. If you are doing this when speaking the local language, you are already part of the performance. If you are doing it as a speaker of English—and almost everywhere in the world you can communicate at a certain basic level of English—you have to hear the English as it is spoken in different cultures.

The intonation of someone from India speaking English may be very different to that of an American from the East Coast or the Pacific Coast, which is again different to the intonation of an Australian or a New Zealander. And let's not even start on the different dialects within Britain—Geordie (Northeast), Scouse (Liverpool), Mancunian (Manchester), Cockney (East London), Brummie (Birmingham), and the many other dialects of England, Scotland, Wales, and Northern Ireland.

Full volume will not help you to communicate with these very different speakers of English. As mentioned earlier, English is a globalized but far from standardized language. In order to get on well with its manifold speakers, you will have to vary your pronunciation and intonation to be understood. You will also have to manage your volume and pitch.

One of Michael's other habits when visiting different countries was to talk too quickly. Not only did he turn up the volume, but also he speeded up what he was saying, or at least he made no attempt to slow down to make sure he was understood. In some way this was a relief, because Michael speaking at full volume *and* slowly would have been very insulting to the other party.

However, his tendency to go at every situation as if he were at home was nevertheless embarrassing—and unhelpful to him. There is no avoiding it. We have to slow down when communicating cross-culturally, even with people who are speaking English.

ROOM FOR THOUGHT

My clarity of enunciation was one of the reasons why my nearest and dearest found my way of speaking amusing after I returned from North America or Asia.

Not only had I unconsciously picked up the grammatical mistakes or turns of phrase of the inhabitants of a particular country or region in the world, I had become used to expressing myself with particular clarity.

This sounds a bit odd for someone whose English was polished at Cambridge University over six or seven years (sadly, removing any Anglo-Welsh musical intonation or expressions in the process). However, I found that speaking English relatively slowly and clearly with the multicultural teams at the international bank was the best way to a) get things done and b) get myself liked.

The latter was crucial. Being liked opened all kinds of doors that speaking in my natural rapid flow did not. Expatriates who gabbled in their own language were not popular with the local Chinese, or Indians, or Filipinos, or Malaysians on the staff. The same applied to the speeches I wrote for Hong Kong's business and government leaders. A local Chinese leader was not likely to rush his English, but a Caucasian leader was very likely to speak too fast.

I spent many an afternoon coaching expatriate executives how to speak with clarity, in short sentences (I wrote those into the speech), with plenty of gaps left for thought or dramatic pauses—anything to vary the tone and make the meaning clear.

This aspect of CQ Action is very important. As the business world becomes more complex, slowing down may seem counter-intuitive. However, a more gentle pace and restrained speech allow time for thought and reflection. This is especially true for cultures and audiences that may well be used to a less frenetic, more relationships-based approach to business.

If you are giving a presentation to an audience that does not speak English as a first language, it doesn't matter how much passion you have for your subject. Slow down, offer shortened sentences and sharper ideas. Keep it relatively simple and leave plenty of time for thought.

SEE THE WORLD DIFFERENTLY

Sometimes I try to imagine how I would see the world without having lived and worked across many different countries. Perhaps I would be a monolingual family lawyer living in a country town in England. Perhaps I would be happy with my lot.

Given my love of other cultures and windows on the world, it's difficult to think I would have been satisfied with a relatively risk-free and culturally unchallenging life. Perhaps the multicultural society that is modern Britain would have reached my country town in the form of immigrant families, European Union workers, and second- or third-generation Britons of ethnically diverse backgrounds.

It's difficult to remain entirely monocultural in the new global economy. Everywhere we look we have friends, colleagues, partners, suppliers, virtual buyers, fellow gym members, club associates from every corner of the world. This could not have been foreseen even twenty years ago.

So I feel extremely fortunate to have had the cultural experiences that have colored and energized my life and work. Probably the biggest influence on both has been the people I have met and who have guided me in the multicultural teams I have been involved with, as well as family and friends from different cultures. Without their help and advice, I would often have been lost.

It is they who enabled me to develop my cultural intelligence. So if you aspire to be a Bamboo Leader, I can think of no better resource than becoming a member of a multicultural team. Some of my most stimulating projects at the international bank were working with members of country teams in Thailand, the Philippines, Japan, and Vietnam, on key messages for their individual markets.

Not only did this work give me a sense of the different approaches to life, attitudes, family customs, and beliefs in each of these countries, I also gained friends who guided me through their cultures and showed me what to do and what to avoid. Working with multicultural teams and on cross-border projects will undoubtedly help you too—even if it's only with simple questions such as how to say yes and no politely, how to defer to the most senior person, when it's your turn to speak in a business meeting, and a thousand other finer points of CQ Action.

Multicultural guides will also help you to avoid blunders or taboos in a particular culture. Some of these taboos may be common sense, such as not photographing or touching an image of Buddha, not putting your feet up in the vicinity of someone's head (especially Thailand), not using your left hand to give a person something or shake hands with in Muslim countries. There are some excellent guides to global business etiquette available on Amazon, and towards the end of this book you can also learn about my own guides to doing business in Asia and China.

However, the Bamboo Leaders of today have to rapidly move in and out of many cultures. They don't have time to master etiquette and taboos for each one. They are more likely to develop a sense for what is appropriate and what is not when they are guided by someone on their team, by a business colleague, partner, or supplier from that local culture.

Being a member of a culturally diverse team allows you to observe how different people behave and react in a similar situation. I have been in many multicultural 'teams' across the globe—including my Swiss-German and Chinese family, my Jewish-American and African-American circle in New York, my Italian farmer community—and in every case I have learned a lot by simply watching and listening.

People of different backgrounds usually give us clues as to how to behave way before they express anything in words. For leaders involved in multicultural projects, this reading of situations and of people is of infinite value. If you simply keep to your circle of People Like Us, you will miss out on this vital opportunity to leverage different viewpoints, different approaches, and different forms of creativity.

To create your own Cultural Intelligence (CQ) Planner, with action points and strategies from this chapter, please visit www.davidcliveprice.com/planner

TRANSFORMATION

WE CAN ALL CHANGE

Did you know that the very dense fibers in each cane of bamboo give the plant extreme flexibility, allowing it to bend without snapping? In earthquakes, a bamboo forest is actually a very safe place to take shelter, and houses made of bamboo have been known to withstand 9.0-magnitude quakes. That is why for thousands of years bamboo has been the go-to building material for most of the world.

Some scientists believe that if bamboo were planted on a mass scale it could completely reverse the effects of global warming in less than a decade. It would also provide a renewable source of food, building material, and erosion prevention.

Trees used for conventional wood take thirty to fifty years to regenerate to their full mass. In the meantime, less oxygen is produced, less carbon dioxide is consumed, and more soil is run off in the spot where the tree is harvested—all producing harmful environmental effects. So when it comes to sustainability, bamboo has traditional lumber beaten in almost every category. Bamboo is clocked as the fastest-growing plant on Earth. Some species have been measured to grow over four feet in twenty-four hours. A pole of bamboo can regenerate to its full mass in just six months! Bamboo can also be continuously re-harvested every three years without causing damage to the plant system and surrounding environment. Continuous harvesting of this woody grass every three to seven years actually improves the overall health of the plant.

I personally witnessed the extraordinary power of the bamboo in the Tuscan valley where I lived. Every time I chopped down a bamboo cane, the same day small green shoots of a new bamboo would appear in the very same spot.

This constant regeneration made me marvel at the strength of nature.

I believe that cultural intelligence has a similar power to grow and change the world. In the thickets of stereotype, indifference, and blind hatred that we see all around us, it is the green shoots of cultural understanding, rapport, and sympathy that have the greatest chance of transforming the globe's political and spiritual ecosystem.

We are living in a period of extreme migrations, of innocent refugees fleeing from political violence, of homelessness, and poverty, and inequality.

People are crossing borders in flight from terrorist groups, from unemployment, and from injustice in numbers that are throwing up isolationists and protectionists as never before. Xenophobia is on the march in many countries of the world.

And yet, we are also living in an age of unprecedented international and multilateral cooperation. Businesses and not-for-profit organizations, educational institutions, and government agencies are collaborating in ways that are unique in history. As the process of globalisation continues, bringing with it special challenges for intercultural understanding, I believe cultural intelligence has a special power to help people change. Companies, business leaders, entrepreneurs, politicians, and academics are all engaged in this process of change and transformation.

And just like the bamboo, which grows in phases marked by stronger circles on the stem, this is a process that can only evolve one step at a time, one cultural encounter at a time, as people reach out and flex their new-found understanding. The four capabilities of cultural intelligence—CQ Drive, CQ Knowledge, CQ Strategy, and CQ Action—are not individual and isolated aspects of our attempt to make the world a better place. They are interrelated stages in the development of our cultural intelligence and of becoming true Bamboo Leaders.

So let's look again at these CQ strategies, to see how they can work together to make people like you and me better citizens of this new global economy.

EXTENDING YOUR REPERTOIRE

The first thing to notice is that the different elements of cultural intelligence can be considered as stand-alone capabilities. You might, for example, be really interested in a particular culture or country (CQ Drive). And yet despite all your learning, reading books, watching movies from that country, and even learning some of the language (CQ Knowledge), you still feel completely out of it.

The only thing I remember of my first trip to Italy as a member of my high school group was being able to read the sign in Italian on the train window—È *vietato sporgersi*. I translated this to mean 'You shouldn't throw yourself out of the window' (it was actually referring to objects like tin cans). When I applied this to my thinking and behaviour around Italians, I was forever imagining that they were about to do something highly emotional—like throwing themselves out of train windows—and that I had better be on my guard.

It took me several more years, two or three more trips to Italy, and a close friendship with another Italian Renaissance scholar, Roberto, to discover a completely different and less volatile Italy than the one of my boyhood imagination (although I still thought that some Italians were too emotional for their own good). It was only when I actually lived in Italy, not so much as a scholar researching in the Archivio di Stato in Modena but as a farmer with a real life in a provincial Italian town, that I took my CQ Drive and CQ Knowledge to the next level of CQ Strategy. This in turn resulted in CQ Action, such as taking part in farmers' dances, exchanging country produce, joining the olive cooperative, and writing a book about my experiences—which took me back to CQ Knowledge!

Simply having knowledge about a country or people's background is not enough to really interact with and learn from that culture. In fact, CQ Knowledge by itself might encourage a coolness and a false sense of control—like some of those academics I knew back in Britain, who studied Italian history but whose feeling for Italy was superior and distant.

On the other hand, books, discussion groups, in-country planning sessions, videoconferences with cross-border teams and functions (CQ Strategy) can all help you prepare for the real engagement of joint projects and for CQ Action.

The interaction of the four capabilities extends your repertoire of responses, behaviors, and ways to communicate with people from another culture. Each capability encourages and reflects on the other, giving you much greater control over your life and work in cross-cultural situations.

THE CQ MODEL

Like the bamboo's cycle of growth, the four capabilities are in a constant state of transformation. It may be comforting to think that our CQ capabilities lead in a logical progression from CQ Drive to CQ Action and are forged together into a kind of permanent, recognizable platform like a hardware operating system or a Ph.D. thesis. But that's not what really happens.

The four stages of cultural intelligence development grow at a different pace and with constant variation.

Sometimes your CQ Drive lacks strength for a particular country or cross-cultural challenge. Sometimes you have far more CQ Knowledge of European markets and cultures, for example, than of Asian or Latin American markets. Sometimes you find yourself leading a multicultural team across different sectors, and you have to work hard not on your CQ Drive and Knowledge but on your CQ Strategy. At another time, CQ Action is required to implement all the information you've been storing in your head about China, or Africa, or the Middle East.

Just as I discovered in Italy, it could well be that your experiences in CQ Action lead you back to new reflections (CQ Knowledge) and changes in behaviour that give you much greater motivation (CQ Drive) for your next cross-cultural challenges. The process is constantly evolving. One of your capabilities may grow more rapidly than the others.

Another of your capabilities may be stuck in paralysis for several years before circumstances drive you to use it in action.

When I first arrived in Japan, I had plenty of CQ Drive to learn about this fascinating country. I also had a little CQ Knowledge gained from books, novels, movies, and a close American writer friend who had lived in Tokyo since 1950.

However, I soon discovered that my CQ Drive and CQ Knowledge were not enough to make me really enjoy living in Tokyo. I would wander around the streets looking at the Japanese and Chinese calligraphy above the shops, and bars, and restaurants as if they were some kind of hieroglyphics in an alien world. I would be attracted to a certain glowing neon sign and yet would be frightened of going in there. I had no idea what would meet me inside or whether I would be immediately ejected as a *gaijin*.

And so I continued to live in Tokyo as if I were looking at the city through a glass screen. I could see what was going on, but I couldn't participate. So I tried out some of my elementary CQ Strategy. I attempted a few words in Japanese, a phrase or two, to see if there was any response— and indeed there was. I soon became a little less of a *gaijin* in my local town and more of a respected visitor. I had a place in society. I existed.

However, this was only the first stage of my CQ Strategy. There was very little activity in the area of my CQ Action beyond the daily exchange of politeness with neighbors and shop owners. My American writer friend, Donald, was an expert on Japanese movies, life, and culture, and had lived in Tokyo since the American occupation. I therefore chose him to be my cross-cultural mentor. It was only when I allowed myself to be guided by him that I really made any progress in my CQ Strategy and CQ Action.

Donald taught me the basics of getting on with the Japanese, the little things that might make a difference in daily life in my corner of Tokyo, the way to be both polite and friendly, the things to avoid, the importance of 'appearances', and many other CQ Action tips.

So by the time I had completed a year in Japan and made my trip all around the country, I had reached a further stage of CQ Knowledge in the form of a book about my travels. I also had developed my CQ Drive, because my experience of Japanese life made me doubly motivated to succeed in Hong Kong.

There is no set process for acquiring perfect cultural intelligence. What may have worked in one encounter may well not work the same way in another culture. What seemed the right strategy in one country may not be effective in another. We are often improvising, thinking on our feet, revising plans, and hopefully reflecting on what we are doing in our new cross-cultural encounters.

However, it is precisely because of these improvised situations, when we are suddenly called upon to react with sensitivity and understanding, that we should have a CQ model in place. The model is as useful in spontaneous situations as it is in planned assignments and projects—such as a merger and acquisition your company is undertaking.

Let's think about that merger idea for a moment. You work for a company based in the United States that has acquired a Singaporean business operating in several Asian countries. There are clearly a number of CQ issues that need to be addressed. Now is the time to consider your CQ model.

Your leadership team could start to think of the four-part process in the following terms:

1. CQ Drive: Are you motivated and ready to work with your new Asian teams in culturally diverse settings? Are you able to work through the explicit or unconscious challenges and conflicts you will probably encounter?

2. CQ Knowledge: Do you really understand the culture and cultural differences of these new markets and how they influence behaviour? This involves knowledge of business and legal systems, family and social values, religious beliefs, as well as rules for verbal and nonverbal behaviour.

3. CQ Strategy: Will you be sufficiently aware of what's happening in these new cross-cultural encounters and able to flex by implementing CQ Knowledge and adapting to new ideas?

4. CQ Action: Will you be ready to focus on the appropriate verbal and physical behaviour for these diverse cross-cultural situations? Are you aware how much this will help you to build trust and respect, and minimize the chances of miscommunication?

This is just one example of the CQ model and how it could help you or your company in a similar situation. There are many other scenarios and an infinite number of solutions.

Nobody ever arrives at a perfect application of the CQ model, or indeed at a fixed point of achievement when all four elements are held in alignment. However, the leaders I have worked with in various parts of the world, and in many different sectors, have found that the CQ model is a vital tool in developing their cultural intelligence and driving up their performance and results.

YIN AND YANG

The Chinese have a saying for the type of businessperson who comes to China intent on doing business in the rational, rules- and law-based way that is common in Western countries. This type of businessperson is usually on a tight schedule, has definite parameters in place for the negotiations they expect to undertake, and considers the sole objective of their visit is to obtain a definitive yes or no to their proposal followed by a binding contract.

The Chinese call such businesspeople 'track-minded Westerners'. They are fond of comparing them to a train tearing down the track that leads in only one direction.

As you can probably guess, these track-minded Westerners are not very popular with the Chinese. Not that the Chinese themselves are averse to results or decisions. It's just that their way of thinking is not dictated by this either/or type of Western logic that can be traced back to the Greek logician and philosopher Aristotle. They see business in more holistic, relationships-based terms. They are less concerned with either/or and more at ease with both/and. They see the various possibilities and even contradictions in a proposal that is held in tension becoming part of the relationship as a whole that gradually unfolds in the future. This type of thinking derives from the ancient Chinese philosophy of Taoism, which is based on a belief in Yin and Yang, the opposing principles of universal harmony that are inextricably intertwined and constantly reconciled.

Much the same can be said for the principles of cultural intelligence. If you are a person who is addicted to either/ or, or thinking in black and white, cultural intelligence may not be for you. You remember the image of the bamboo with its tensile strength and flexibility? Much cultural intelligence work is based on your ability to hold two viewpoints, or maybe even several viewpoints, in creative tension at the same time.

These viewpoints could be: We have to make smart informed decisions; we have to build slowly through relationships. We have to speak the basics of the Japanese language; we can get further by speaking English and playing the outsider. We have to promote our global brand; we have to adapt to local tastes and needs. We have a common humanity; we have to learn and respect cultural differences. We have to strengthen our global organizational culture; we have to leverage our local diversity.

These contradictions or complementary viewpoints are not a bad thing.

It is obvious that in dealing with people of so many cultures and backgrounds, we are going to encounter gaps in understanding, tensions, or conflicts of various kinds. But we should see them as a cause for celebration rather than a reason for complaining. The clash and mesh of different viewpoints encourage innovation. People bring different ideas and approaches to the table, there is discussion and disagreement, and often there is a creative solution.

It is a strange paradox of our times—another cultural paradox we have to live with—that the more fundamentalist groups exert their poisonous influence in the world, the more we are ready to connect with cultures and peoples from many different backgrounds and approaches to life. To some extent this is due to the prevalence of the Internet. But it's also due to increased travel by every generation, access to new markets, migration patterns, and simply the increasingly multicultural nature of the workplace.

Just as an educated young Chinese may now show intense curiosity about British, American, or European culture, and possibly live and work in those regions of the world, so too may a European or American person be fascinated by China and Chinese culture, and possibly live and work in China. In both instances, this curiosity will override possible skepticism about each country's political systems or 'national mission'.

This is a simplistic example, but there is some truth behind it. CQ encourages complex thinking, which includes the possibility of holding two or more diverging viewpoints within us at the same time: the Yin and Yang, or the both/and principle of Taoist thought. Fundamentalism, on the other hand, insists that one way is the only right way and there is no other possible point of view.

The more the world becomes accessible, the more viewpoints we have to take into consideration and hold in creative tension. This does not mean we have to lose our identity or our authenticity. However, it is possible that sometimes we have to flex, to become almost another person, or at least to put ourselves in another's position and imagine how they are feeling.

This can do nothing but good for our mental growth and our spiritual wellbeing. When so much of the global news agenda is asking us to be this or that, to have this or that final view on pretty much everything that goes on in the world, it is salutary to have a reason to stop, reflect, compare, and feel the richness of possible diverging views. All human life is like that. It shouldn't be too much of a jump to develop our cultural intelligence in the same way.

When all's said and done, people are complex. That is why the advice of intercultural books on specific countries, although often helpful, should also be observed as guidance only rather than as rigid rules of how people behave in different cultures. There are many exceptions to national traits, and we have to remember that everyone is individual, wherever they are from, and everyone is constantly developing or changing their viewpoints.

The benefit of the CQ model is that it will allow you to reflect and act on these evolving points of view, even when they conflict with your own.

STANDING BACK A MOMENT

It is not easy to find time to reflect in this increasingly frenetic era of smart phones and snap decisions, sudden disruptions in the marketplace, new modes of communication, and the daily deluge of information and emails. Standing back a moment is almost a quaint tradition of a past when people went to church and sat in pews to reflect, or trekked up mountainsides, or made a quiet excursion to a beach to watch the waves ebb and flow.

I hope this book has given you an opportunity to reflect on your life and career, and on the value of cultural intelligence or CQ in an ever more connected and yet complex world. It has been exciting and inspiring to take you on this journey, into which I have poured all my expertise and experience in many cultures to assist you along the way. The scientifically tested CQ model has helped many companies, organisations, and not-for-profits all around the world in a huge variety of ways. Some organisations have adopted cultural intelligence on an ad hoc basis for specific marketing and branding initiatives, global talent management programs, educational and development projects, negotiation strategies, and mergers and acquisitions.

Others such as Accenture, BMW, BNP Paribas, Coca-Cola, Google, Harvard Business School, Hilton Hotels, IBM, London School of Economics, Novartis, NTT, Shangri-La Hotels, the United Nations, and many more organisations in a wide spectrum of industries across more than ninety countries have embraced cultural intelligence as an integral part of their work and as a means to raise the global effectiveness of their workforce.

Having been an academic myself and broken free of the shackles of academe, I have sometimes been slightly skeptical of scholarly discoveries. However, the findings of CQ research over the past decade or more have been truly revolutionary. Cultural intelligence has not only helped many large organisations but also entrepreneurs, teachers, coaches, consultants, artists, musicians, expatriates, and diplomats assimilate into new postings overseas, improve their lives, and make the world a better place.

I have an Australian friend who lives in Vietnam and operates a network he calls Corporate Cultural Diplomacy, which promotes the brand and profile of companies and organisations all across Asia through staging cultural events in different Asian countries based on cultural intelligence.

CQ helps such companies build a sustainable business that captures as many customers as possible and offers them products that celebrate both the culture of the company's own country and that of the host country.

I hope the stories and examples in this book will give you the inspiration to build new relationships, communicate, network, negotiate, and lead in culturally diverse workplaces all across our globalized world—including virtual teams. Whether adapting global business models for local markets, opening new markets, seeking a diverse customer base, or negotiating with international suppliers, developed CQ can make all the difference between success and failure.

YOU ARE NOT ALONE

CQ offers us the ability not only to stand back and think before and after each cultural encounter, but also to reflect while we are in the middle of new experiences and challenges. It allows us to engage with a problem in three dimensions, looking at it from all sides and creating possible solutions as we go.

If you have taken any benefit from this book, I hope it is in seeing a path towards developing your own cultural intelligence. Clearly, books like this are by their nature general. You will have your own cross-cultural challenges that are specific to you or your organisation. However, having come this far, I am fairly sure you will be interested to know how problems that are perhaps similar to yours are met and solved—especially how they are solved in a systematic, inspired way by the application of CQ.

I am fortunate that in my cultural intelligence work around the world I encounter so many fascinating and highly motivated individuals and organisations. Since 1995, I have helped business leaders, multicultural teams, international negotiators, and other global executives accomplish their goals, drive performance, and maximize profits in a broad variety of cultural environments.

One day I may be working with a Canadian insurance multinational aiming to adapt its leadership team to the new challenges of operating in Latin America. Another day I'm helping to establish a cultural intelligence programme in the global network of a financial institution based in London. On another day I may be working with the Sri Lankan government to develop programmes for its international export and foreign investment projects. Or I might be delivering virtual workshops for the sales teams of a San Francisco company expanding into Asia.

Together with these Bamboo Leaders and their teams, I work through a variety of cultural scenarios and situations, so that their cultural intelligence becomes a natural, instinctive part of their leadership skills.

I guide them through the first phases of CQ Drive by introducing them to a Cultural Intelligence (CQ) Planner, so that together with their colleagues or line managers they can prepare themselves for proceeding to the next stages of the CQ model. Once these findings are delivered and interpreted, we move on to interactive workshops and modules created for their specific challenges with CQ Knowledge and CQ Strategy, before gathering all our learning together in CQ Action plans and deliverables.

One of the most effective ways to build cultural intelligence into an organisation is for Bamboo Leaders to cascade their learning down into the teams in their home office. By sharing the CQ model with others, leaders learn more about the four capabilities and develop each one further.

CQ is in essence a group-centered learning experience that is being constantly challenged and upgraded. Participants in the basic four steps of the system report a sharp increase in business innovation in their companies, which translates into increased profitability as well as a marked improvement in continuous learning and leadership agility.

RISING TO MEET THE FUTURE

There are certain moments in life that have a special resonance, a strange sense of the universe telling you something. I recently experienced such a moment when I returned to Hong Kong and found myself speaking in a conference room full of delegates from some forty countries from around the globe—including a dozen or so Asian countries.

The first part of my Bamboo Strong presentation begins with a story: I am standing on the twenty-eighth floor of the international bank I worked for in the run-up to the return of Hong Kong to China. I am feeling stressed from so many briefings and strategy meetings and speech deadlines. As I look out of my office window across Victoria Harbour, I realize that I've seen almost nothing of the real life of Hong Kong since I arrived in the colony a few weeks earlier. It's been all expatriate restaurants and bars, returning exhausted to my temporary shared apartment in the Mid-Levels area of Hong Kong, meetings with senior management and phone conferences with the London team. I have barely made any Chinese friends and know nothing of what goes on in the rest of Hong Kong outside the Central business district.

Just then Cindy Wong, one of my few Chinese friends in the bank, knocks on my door and enters. Seeing me staring out of the window, she asks me, 'Is there anything wrong?'

'I've got cabin fever,' I say, turning to face her. 'I can't seem to get out of here. I don't know what Hong Kong's all about.'

'Oh, I see,' she says. 'Well, I think I've got the answer for you. I'm going with a group of friends to the New Territories on Saturday. Do you want to come?'

'Of course,' I say. 'What are we going to do?' 'We're going to the Cantonese opera.'

My heart sinks. I try not to show it, but from what I've seen of Cantonese opera on late night television, it's an awful squeaky sort of thing with interminable scenes that seem to go on all night.

'Great!' I lie. 'That sounds fantastic.'

So Saturday comes, and I go out to the New Territories to meet the others with a heavy sense of foreboding. I am wondering how on earth I can get out of it. It's going to be an excruciating bore—of that I'm certain.

How wrong I am. Almost from the very moment the curtain goes up on the bamboo stage in the square, I am entranced: Fantastic make-up, weird headgear and flamboyant costumes, lots of scheming and head-twitching, a series of kung fu fights, spears being twirled, drums beaten, the snarl of reed pipes, the crash of cymbals. By the time we reach the end of the first act and go to dinner, I have taken my first big step into Chinese life—and into a new realm of cultural intelligence. Later that same night, as I am telling Cindy about my excitement, she introduces me to Simon…

As we reached the end of this story, I saw the faces of the audience light up with recognition or amusement, and I realized I had hit the spot. How many people find it difficult to get out and into new cultures because they have all kinds of preconceptions and stereotypes to wade through before they get there? Cultural intelligence shows them how to bridge that gap.

Sometimes we have these odd moments in life when we seem to have come full circle, when some special coincidence makes us see things or ourselves more clearly. Just at that moment in Hong Kong I thought that I had completed that circle: speaking to an international audience about the cultural intelligence I had first begun to develop right there some twenty years earlier.

CQ is a journey—that's what I discovered when I further honed my capabilities in Hong Kong and in other locations in Asia. You can either follow the journey to meet the future or you can remain imprisoned in your own world as I was before the night at the Cantonese opera.

It's up to you. The world is changing at an unprecedented pace. Will you change with it? Or will you remain enclosed, confused, overwhelmed, and stressed in your own silo?

If you want to become a true Bamboo Leader, there are two options for reaching your goal. You can visit me at www. davidcliveprice.com/planner to tell me about your multicultural experiences and download a free Cultural Intelligence (CQ) Planner to get you started. Or if you'd like to speak with me directly about how cultural intelligence can help you or your organisation, please contact me at info@david-cliveprice.com or call +44 (0) 77 6633 5805.

It's up to all of us to spread the message on how to make the world a better place. If you've found the contents of this book stimulating, please feel free to recommend it to others like yourselves and encourage them to get in contact with me if they're ready to begin their cultural intelligence journey to meet the future.

To create your own Cultural Intelligence (CQ) Planner, with action points and strategies from this chapter, please visit www.davidcliveprice.com/planner

A (NOT QUITE) FINAL WORD

You Too Can Be a Bamboo Leader

I have tried to give you the insights, the strategies, and above all the personal motivation to develop the mindset of a modern and sophisticated Bamboo Leader. I have never been fully convinced of the term 'Zeitgeist' (literally 'spirit of the times') to explain dramatic or coincidental changes in the tide of human affairs. A Zeitgeist is too broad a definition to include all the complexities, anomalies, and contradictions of human behaviour, or of national, social, or cultural movements.

However, it seems to me that we are living in a time when there is a definite groundswell, a clash of ideologies, between those who view greater cultural understanding and intelligence as an enormous benefit to mankind and those who would retreat into the bunkers of intolerance, stereotype, and xenophobia.

This type of thinking poses a false dichotomy. As I have shown you in this book, you can become a Bamboo Leader without losing your sense of self or the authenticity of your own beliefs and customs. Indeed, by being true to yourself and your own culture, you will create the confidence to absorb the richness of other cultures. I believe this is a moment in history to celebrate the intermingling of peoples and races that even a few decades ago would have been unimaginable.

This is particularly true in the world of business, but it is also true in almost everything we do. Due to the opening up of so many markets, the super-connectivity we experience daily, and the changing balance in the global economic system, we have a unique opportunity to reach out, be curious, learn, adapt, and richly benefit from a position of strength—not of weakness.

I read recently that my own university of Cambridge is taking more than eight hundred new undergraduate students from China every year. Many thousands of Chinese visitors now travel annually to Cambridge to visit a meadow near King's College and pay homage at a stone inscribed by the Chinese poet Xu Zhimo, whose poems about Cambridge in the 1920s are now part of China's national educational curriculum.

This is just a small example of cross-cultural inspiration. If so many Chinese are learning about Cambridge and visiting the city, we should also be learning about Hangzhou (with its beautiful West Lake) or about the great Tang dynasty poet, Li Bai, the 'drunken poet'. Not for the sake of it, not to be clever, but because we can discover something new about each other's thinking, aspirations, and culture.

Although this is the end of this book, that doesn't mean it has to be the end of our work together. In the preceding chapters, I have given you a series of insights and action steps through the Cultural Intelligence (CQ) Planner to guide you to greater personal fulfillment and wealth. Have you referred to these steps throughout the book? If you have, that's a life-changer, so keep at it. If you haven't, how about starting to practice them right now? Your success directly corresponds to the actions you take.

To this end, you can continue to obtain advice and support about all the strategies I've discussed in this book at www.davidcliveprice.com. If you want more help, then join me on one of my virtual Bamboo Strong™ learning courses, attend a live speaking event near you, or work directly with me in my personal mentoring programs.

I am honoured that you have taken time out of your schedule to read my book and listen to my guidance. Developing your cultural intelligence will make your world fresher, more vibrant, and more alive. I want to continue to serve you and help you to achieve all your dreams, hopes, and goals. I also would like you to share with me your stories of achievement and let you read about others at my website.

In whichever way we share, I very much look forward to meeting and greeting YOU and to helping you on your journey to becoming a true Bamboo Leader.

And if there is anything I can do to be of service, please just ask.

David Clive Price
www.davidcliveprice.com
info@davidcliveprice.com

HOW TO REACH
DAVID CLIVE PRICE

Participate in a Bamboo Strong™ Training Course, Workshop or Mentoring Programme

These are vibrant, kick-start, inspirational events and courses that will challenge your normal patterns of thinking and feeling and provide you with a comprehensive system to enrich your business and your life.

Learn more at http://www.davidcliveprice.com

Bamboo Strong programmes: http://www.davidcliveprice.com/coaching

The *Bamboo Strong* book gift bonus: http://www.davidcliveprice.com/planner

David speaks: http://www.davidcliveprice.com/global-leadership-speaker

David coaches: http://www.davidcliveprice.com/coaching

The Age of Pluralism book also by David Clive Price: http://www.davidcliveprice.com/leadership-topics.

The Master Key to Asia book also by David Clive Price: http://www.davidcliveprice.com/master-key-asia

The Master Key to China book also by David Clive Price: http://www.davidcliveprice.com/master-key-china

SPEAKING

To discuss David's availability for speaking at your live event or for interviews on telesummits, podcasts, in print or on live media, please email us with your requirements to info@davidcliveprice.com
Follow David on Twitter: @davidcliveprice
Join David on LinkedIn: https://uk.linkedin.com/in/davidcliveprice

Become a Bamboo Leader
Thousands of executives, business owners, and professionals have achieved success thanks to the advice and systems in this book. You can too.

ABOUT THE AUTHOR

David Clive Price, Ph.D.
International Bestselling Author and Speaker

David Clive Price is the author of *The Age of Pluralism* and is a highly sought-after speaker who inspires and entertains audiences all over the world with his acclaimed Bamboo Strong™ keynotes and programs using Cultural Intelligence (CQ).

In addition to speaking, David devotes much of his time to developing masterminds, facilitating leadership retreats and coaching CEOs, business leaders, and their teams.

His multicultural and interactive keynotes have inspired audiences from Australia, Denmark, Hong Kong, The Netherlands, New Zealand and Singapore, to the United Kingdom and the United States.

Building on his own learning as chief speechwriter and cultural integration specialist for HSBC, he has coached and advised leadership teams for many global organizations including AIA, Standard Chartered, Credit Suisse, Santander, Julius Baer and Morgan Stanley as well as political and trade leaders.

Speaking English, French, German, Italian and Cantonese, and having lived and worked in numerous countries, David's multicultural experience informs all his executive coaching, as well as his bestselling book *The Age of Pluralism* with foreword by John Mattone.

He is a visiting lecturer on global leadership at the University of Greenwich Business School, holds a Ph.D. in Renaissance History from Cambridge University, and often appears in the media, including BBC Radio, The Wall Street Journal, Business Insider, and International Business Times.

He is the author of four books on international business and leadership, including *The Age of Pluralism* (2019) *The Master Key to Asia* (2013) and *The Master Key to China* (2014).

After living for twenty-five years in Italy, Switzerland, Hong Kong, Japan, South Korea, the United Kingdom, and the United States, he is now based in London, where he lives with his husband.

Find out more and connect with David via his website: http://www.davidcliveprice.com

For More News About David Clive Price,
Signup For Our Newsletter:

http://wbp.bz/newsletter

Word-of-mouth is critical to an author's long-term success. If you appreciated this book please leave a review on the Amazon sales page:

http://wbp.bz/bamboostronga

THE AGE OF PLURALISM by DAVID CLIVE PRICE

http://wbp.bz/aopa

Read A Sample Next

1. TRIBAL TOM-TOMS

Tribalism: a very strong feeling of loyalty to a political or social group, so that you support them whatever they do (Cambridge Dictionary)

I was sitting in the coffee bar of my local gym the day after the wedding of Meghan Markle to Prince Harry and discussing the wedding coverage in the newspapers with Dev, a member of my gym class.

Dev is of Indian descent but he has lived all his life in London, and he works for a big legal firm as a strategic advisor.

'It's all a bit overblown,' said Dev. 'I mean, yes, she has a black mother and a white father, but it's not as if racial discrimination is going to die out overnight just because they've got hitched.'

'No', I said, 'that's very true. But the media have painted it as a symbol of changing times—and I have to say they have a point.'

Dev looked at me quizzically, as if I didn't quite understand the issues at stake. Then he smiled. 'Something tells me you are a true Brit—queen and country and all that. A bit of a royalist?'

I laughed. It was true I did have a sneaking admiration for things royal, history, and traditions, ever since I was a boy. I rather liked pomp and ceremony, at least the way Brits did them (and the French too), and I had studied kings and queens and courts for my history degree.

So yes, I had enjoyed the Royal Wedding—but just as much for what it represented as for what actually took place. It didn't move me because it was royal and British and confirmed my tribal identity.

It moved me because it was interracial and celebratory of mixed heritage. There was a black gospel choir from London singing the spiritual 'This Little Light of Mine'. There was a rousing, evangelist-style sermon from a senior American black bishop, quoting Martin Luther King Jr. There was young, award-winning black cellist Sheku Kanneh-Mason playing Fauré.

And most of all, there was an American actress bride of mixed heritage supported by her cool and elegant mother Doria. And all this within St. George's Chapel at Windsor Castle, attended by the cream of the British establishment.

'But it's not just me, Dev. I think a lot of people liked it, not because it celebrated Britishness. But because the mixed race thing was no big deal. It was kind of, well, normal.'

'Mmmm,' said Dev. 'Let's see how that pans out. One mixed race royal marriage is not going to solve racial discrimination all in one go. People are still going to stick to their tribes.'

'That's true,' I said. 'But most people were more interested in her dress and outfits than her skin colour—isn't that's a sign of progress? I mean, maybe we're starting to grow up. Maybe we're ready to stop defining people simply by what they look like.'

'Or by the tribes they belong to,' said Dev and took a long meaningful sip of his coffee.

In the following days I thought a lot about Dev and that comment about tribes. And I did some research.

It turned out that he was right. According to Trevor Phillips, former chairman of the UK Equality and Human Rights Commission, Britain is now the western country in which interracial marriages are most common. There are more than 1 million dual-heritage Brits, the largest single group being the children of white Brits and people of African or Caribbean descent. By 2030, if the term 'black British' is ever used, it is more likely to mean mixed race. The usual tribal epithets will become irrelevant.

So maybe I was right too. The wedding of Prince Harry and Meghan Markle showed that mixed-race marriages aren't exceptional. Indeed, the problem with dividing the world into tribes is that it leaves out these essential drivers of modern life. In a unique way, the children of mixed marriages combine two different worlds, increasingly at ease in all parts of society rather than being identified by their skin colour or tribe.

We are not defined by simple labels or movements or assumed loyalties. We are not one thing or another. Whatever the politicians and social media and pundits might say, we are not black and white, not even physically. And we cannot hope to influence, guide, and collaborate with other people-especially in our incredibly interconnected world-if we rely on tribal allegiances and readymade categories.

Today's global economy is far too fast moving and fluid to be divided into tribes. However much populist movements and protectionists, nationalists, and nativists try to divide the world based on identity-into tribes of 'them' and 'us', countries and groups, races and religions, local and global-they cannot hold back the tide of pluralism that is sweeping the globe.

And in order to ride this wave, leaders must be able to embrace complexity and change, reach out to other viewpoints and perspectives, and learn to create new combinations and richer amalgams of thought and action.

Most commentators misunderstand the nature of tribes. Their view of them as primitive and insular, even violent, is common in the vocabulary of modern politics. It's as if the recourse to tribalism is some ancient mechanism, a return to an ancestral way of doing things. In our vague anthropology, we think of tribes as imposing unity on individuals by repetitive social customs. Contemporary tribes such as political parties are seen as a natural refuge from inevitable conflict. They are exclusionary and conformist, offering safety in numbers and an admiration of authoritarianism. They believe in their moral superiority.

But as many anthropological studies show, actual tribes are characterized by surprisingly open boundaries. They experiment with other tribes' practices and social forms. They frequently adopt outsiders. Captured white settlers were often invited into the communal life of North American tribes (even staying in the group when liberated). Among certain tribes in North Africa, members can voluntarily leave their own tribe and join another.

Traditional tribesmen continually create forms of mutual obligation, not only within the tribe but also across tribes. Leaders of the Berbers of North Africa, for example, are commonly chosen or ratified by the group's opponents in the belief that one's current enemy may later be an ally.

Imagine the Republicans and Democrats in the USA choosing the other party's leaders! What would happen if members of the populist right wing and left wing parties of Europe changed loyalties every so often? Many tribes, such as the Mae Enga of Papua New Guinea and the Lozi of Central Africa, even share the practice of marrying members of enemy tribes to reduce the possibility of inter-tribal warfare. Grandchildren are raised in different kinship groups, and a majority of tribes are multilingual due to intermarriage and strong trading relations.

Tribes do not need to be exclusionary to flourish. You might draw parallels with contemporary educational exchange between countries like China and the USA, or the incubator startups and digital entrepreneurs of Bangalore or Silicon Valley or Shanghai. These open groups are much more like traditional tribes in the sense of being built on the cross-fertilization of ideas. They are inherently non-authoritarian, inclusive, and loosely democratic.

The partisan tribes of our contemporary politics are mainly characterized by aggression and, above all, a sense of moral superiority. This is in direct contrast to historical tribes. Most of these groups, as the anthropologist Paul Dresch says of Yemeni tribes, practice an 'avoidance of any absolute judgment, a kind of moral particularism or pluralism.' This is because traditional tribes know that social isolation or claims of moral superiority limit their flexibility. They must be able to adapt to survive. They cannot adapt if they are exclusive, or if they have a rigid set of rules for every situation.

Present day identity politics borrows the warring images of tribes to make our politics much more adversarial than necessary. It seals tribal members off from other tribes and, more damagingly, from the diversity and accelerating technological change that is the reality for thousands of intermingling cultures across the globe. Rather than cutting people off from each other and seeking security in smaller groups-as our current political tribes attempt-we should be embracing the opportunities of collaboration, innovation, and creativity that the global economy presents.

Whether we like it or not, we are now more interconnected than ever before, and we have far less scope for thinking of people far away as 'not like us' or worse, 'stupid'. All the peoples of the world are teaching each other new perspectives, different visions, unexpected connections on a daily basis. You may think of yourself a being part of the post-globalisation wave. You may consider yourself a member of a tribe that has been left behind by the rising tide of globalisation. You may even be anti-globalist.

It doesn't matter. Whether your tribe is for or against globalisation, we are all global citizens now. Rather than seeing the world in terms of tribal or nationalist loyalties, it is much more productive-and tribal in the traditional sense-to think of yourself as a global citizen.

This does not mean that you are a 'citizen of nowhere', as British prime minster Theresa May once declared in relation to international business élites. It does mean that you are plugged into the cultures, perspectives, and customs of people of many backgrounds all across the world. You may be following them on the Internet or via streaming devices. You may be doing business with them. They may be part of your international or virtual team. They may be just round the corner or at the farthest end of the globe. You may access them via translation apps, or simply in the lingua franca of English, Spanish, or Chinese via Skype or Zoom.

However you relate to them, they are part of your daily world and business life. Thinking in purely 'tribal' terms means that you are almost certainly missing out on vast areas of experience and abundance that this extraordinary wired planet of ours now offers. Get over the old tribalism-which is, in fact, a caricature of tribalism. Become a leader in the borderless world that is now at your fingertips!

The leaders of the future must look beyond tribes and borders. They must cultivate an inner curiosity and malleability to thrive in many different cultural situations, and with people of many different backgrounds. When Berber tribes find themselves in a dispute, one group may call on the leader of the other to settle the claim, in the knowledge that he will not risk his ability to form later alliances by supporting his own side.

Now that's what I call global leadership.

2. THE RISE OF THE AMPHIBIANS

Looking back, I guess I always thought of myself as a bit of an amphibian. In every place and culture I went, I sank or swam—and usually swam.

According to the dictionary, the literal definition of amphibian is 'a cold-blooded vertebrate animal of a class that comprises the frogs, toads, newts, salamanders, and caecilians. They are distinguished by having an aquatic gill-breathing larval stage followed typically by a terrestrial lung-breathing adult stage.'

I am not cold blooded (I hope), nor have I moved from breathing through gills to breathing through lungs. But the broader sense of the word, derived from the Greek word amphibious, suggests having two lives or living in both water and on land. This is borne out by the modern adaptation of the noun 'amphibian', meaning a vehicle that is able to move on both land and water, or an aeroplane that can land on both land and water.

So my metaphor of sinking or swimming is reasonably accurate. My parents were born in Wales but I was born in London, so nothing very exotic there. Perhaps I first learned to sink or swim as a 17-year-old grammar school boy going up to Cambridge University, where I found myself surrounded by more mature public school boys. They already had cosmopolitan airs and had the money to travel in their summer vacations.

It was only when I was well into my postgraduate studies that I met my first partner, who happened to be Swiss German. So on finishing my doctorate, I made a big decision. I went to live with Davide and his family in Switzerland—which is when my amphibian instincts took over. I learned Swiss German to converse with my family while I also improved my French. Under the influence of the Swiss Sprachwunder (language miracles) all around me, I also learned rudimentary Italian and helped Davide organize a film festival every year in Locarno, in the Italian part of Switzerland.

From Locarno it seemed just a short step into Italy itself. I was lucky. I managed to obtain a British Academy Travel Fellowship at the University of Bologna, and then went on to lecture on Renaissance history at the European Institute in Florence. Nothing seemed to stop me exploring at that age. Nothing seems to stop young people now, who are, if anything, more amphibious than me. I lived for a while in a converted garage near Bologna station (convenient for trains to the archives in Modena and Mantua). And then together with Davide, I bought a broken-down farmhouse in Tuscany and for a while, I commuted to Florence, while I worked the land for wine and olives, Davide commuted to Locarno, and I began to write my first novel.

It all seemed to happen naturally somehow. One moment I was studying in the cloistered halls of Cambridge University and the next I was a farmer and writer in Italy. And it didn't end there. In order to research that first novel,

I eventually decided to take a year off from Tuscany and travel to New York. There I rented a cheap apartment just south of the downtown area of Manhattan called Alphabet City (Avenues A to C). At that time in the early 1980s, the streets to the south of East Houston Street were not entirely safe, but they hosted a richly diverse and not-yet-gentrified sub-culture in which citizens of every race and nation on Earth were gathered in close proximity. Rich terrain to set a novel.

Indeed, New York gave me confidence to celebrate being amphibious, while also giving me the freedom to be creative alongside people from many different backgrounds- Jews, blacks, Hispanics, Eastern Europeans, Chinese, Koreans- who I met there and who seemed to be as amphibious as I was. Perhaps it was no surprise that I met and fell in love with an African American painter while I lived in Alphabet City. My passion was not reciprocated and by the time I returned to Italy, my decade-long relationship with Davide was seriously damaged. It took us another two years to split. I stayed on at the farm to write my book and then Davide encouraged me to seek new pastures in a region of the world that was already fascinating me.

Instead of returning to England, I headed for Tokyo. And then, after a year of finding that I was more sinking than swimming, I followed Davide's generous advice and moved to Hong Kong.

Arriving in this British colony with nothing much more than a PhD and a couple of published books in my luggage, I found work as a economics researcher for the Economist Intelligence Unit. After a couple of years finding my feet, I successfully applied for the position of speechwriter for HSBC, one of the world's leading banks. My remit was to create the key messages for the handover of Hong to China in July 1997. I also met Simon, a young Hong Kong Chinese man who was in a group of friends who came to the airport to greet me on my arrival from Tokyo. I have been together with him ever since.

So yes, I became an Asian amphibian. In order to explore my new family and their culture, I lived together with Simon's mother, sister, and nephew in their small apartment in a Kowloon housing estate. In that way I really got to know about Chinese daily life, festivals, and customs, even as I took a taxi each morning to work in the shiny HSBC headquarters in the Central financial district.

One of the big benefits of being in a multinational was that I could continue my work as a freelance writer in my spare time and long vacations. So I travelled extensively in South Korea, Japan, Myanmar, China, Thailand, all the while writing books and articles. Throughout this period I also continued to adopt the same amphibious approach as I had in Europe: Swim, David! Don't sink!

Indeed, I have continued to live like this ever since: being ready to explore in a new culture, having one foot here and one foot there, getting adopted by locals or even a whole family. In so doing, I have often found myself an outsider, on the edge of a culture where I can communicate both ways— into and out of the group. But whereas I once thought I was one of a lucky few who sought out these hybrid experiences, now I think it is quite commonplace.

This is especially true of the young leaders and potential leaders of today. It's amazing how many millennials now seem to be of mixed background. I've lost count of the number of people who tell me they are Third Culture Kids or TCKs. This term, first used by sociologist Ruth Hill Useem in the 1950s for children raised in a culture other than their parents' (or the culture of a country given on a child's passport), has become a mark of pride for many people of mixed parentage.

I was recently coaching an executive who was brought up in his father's native country of Brazil. He speaks Portuguese and English, but currently lives in California near his mother, managing two trading teams in Singapore and Malaysia. He calls himself a TCK and was rather aggrieved that he wasn't getting the results he deserved from his Southeast Asia teams, 'even though I am used to adapting to other cultures.'

I have another colleague, Eric, who is married to a Japanese woman, but who spent several years in Shanghai and has a Chinese mother and a French father. He speaks Mandarin, French, and English, and now lives and works in London and New York. His children speak English, French, and Mandarin. Perhaps unsurprisingly, he is an expert in international start-ups.

This amphibiousness seems to have become more marked as the pace of technological change, international travel, interracial marriage, matrix working, and social media quickens. Not only is everyone connected, but also several life experiences are connected within one person or one family.

Amphibians are pluralism personified. However, pluralism isn't just living with difference, or tolerating difference, or even celebrating difference. It's discovering that you have roots here but also there, a dynamic that creates a third personality. 'Being hyphenated can sometimes cause problems,' one TCK told me. 'But it's also fun.'

I am not officially hyphenated but my hybrid experiences have made a coherent identity of all my influences. Of course it might not be so much fun for others, such as expatriate executives, who are sometimes relocated time and again because they haven't been able to work in the prevailing culture.

I can think of many people in the multinationals where I've worked, or executive clients who have been discomfited by new cultural situations, new members of their international teams, or new in-country assignments where they simply have not 'gelled'. Failing in Japan or Saudi Arabia or Mexico (or on the East and West Coasts of the US) costs companies huge amounts of money in replacement costs and also in repatriating disgruntled executives, who may well leave the company in the aftermath of disappointment.

Research shows that some 65 per cent of expatriates fail in the first or second posting, while 90 per cent of global executives identify cross-cultural effectiveness as their biggest challenge.

Clearly, there are many professionals out there who are non-amphibians. However, the more you look around the more you see examples of interesting and hybrid backgrounds, especially among the often well-travelled and footloose younger generation. These are our future leaders. And although they may not be ready for leadership yet, many of them are already tending towards that edge-of-the-group mindset and appreciation of mixed influences where creativity flourishes. If you look at Western media, TV, and films-or even Japanese, Korean, or Latin American media and films-you will see mixed race, mixed sexuality, and mixed backgrounds portrayed on the screen now far more than ever before.

Our Master Chef and Celebrity Bake-off programmes on UK television are full of exotic 'fusion' dishes from cuisines all over the world. The contestants are British-born Somalis and Nigerians, Indians, Chinese, Sri Lankans, Columbians, Cypriots, Italians, and many others of diverse backgrounds. It's perhaps no surprise that it is these contestants who are often the most creative.

But what really makes an amphibian succeed? What makes one person flourish in diverse situations and cultures, some of them far removed from anything they have experienced before, while another is like a fish out of water? What are the main drivers that are making the amphibians thrive with every fresh experience of difference?

http://wbp.bz/aopa

Chapter One

Live, Immaterial, and Functional

Since the time of Cicero, people have tended to take the phenomenon of culture for granted, often assuming that it is synonymous with organizational culture. However, a more specialized understanding of organizational culture began to coalesce some decades ago. In fact, it was first described as a group climate by Lewin, Lippitt, and White in 1939. Subsequently, in the mid-seventies, organizational norms, roles, and values were viewed in terms of the social psychology of organizations, although, at that stage, it was not explicitly stated as organizational climate or culture. Since then, a large number of definitions have appeared, serving to confirm the complex nature of this incorporeal being. However, we are still exploring this elephant in a dark room.

Culture does not exist in an isolated and purified environment without the presence of other people. Culture is a complex phenomenon, deeply interpenetrating all of our daily activities, which exists only in collectives of people, i.e. in states, nations, and organizations. Culture is a system itself. The word "system" derives from the ancient Greek word *systema* which comes from two words – *syn*, which means "together", and *histemi*, which means "to set." System is actually an idea which defines how process or ideology is to be set for the best possible performance or outcome. Cultural or ideological systems can be seen as a collection of roles which reflect human values and thus have a direct impact on organizational results. As a system, culture needs to be viewed using a systematic approach and not a mono-dimensional view.

Three Dimensions of Culture

Culture is multidimensional. One dimension is pragmatic and rational, regulating rules, norms, and codes of working in organizations. A second dimension is more irrational and incorporates the behavioral and psychological approach of the group's members to their duties and to the organization itself. A third dimension reflects the transcendent side of culture, which can be viewed as the organizational cathedral, the reference point for the entire organization's activity.

Regarding the strictly rational aspect, Aristotle wisely defined a state, as an interaction for reaching mutual goals. Not short-term tasks, but goals of successful survival, prosperity, mutual support, defense, and satisfaction of its own needs. Applying Aristotle's definition to an organizational viewpoint, we can say that it is similar to the purpose of the state, just on a smaller scale – an organization is the interaction of its members ordered to reach defined goals that benefit the organization.

Organisational Anatomy (Konovalov 2016, 71) defines organizational culture as a catalyzer of performance. I will use this definition in the present discussion as being the most advanced and practically relevant to the aims of all organizations. Looking at the spiritual or transcendent side, we can consider company culture as the soul of the organizational body, which helps the brain (management) motivate the body for action, sense the environment, attract stakeholders' positive emotions and energy, stimulate and encourage development, and drive the organization through tough times.

This third dimension is the dynamic power and spiritual core of the organization. It is built on symbols which shape the company's psychological state and define the boundaries of its influence. We will discuss the role of symbols and values in more detail later as this is a tremendously critical and under-appreciated issue.

Each of these facets of organizational culture empowers and enlightens the other sides of the immaterial core of any company, and by doing so, gives life and vitality to a company. Culture also defines the boundaries of an organization. Within those boundaries, dependent upon the culture's nature, the talents of the employees are revealed and allowed to flourish.

Indispensable Catalyzer

Production or providing of services can be compared with a complicated chemical reaction of long-chain utilization of resources by perfectly synergized functions. A chemical reaction is a change of two components – substance and energy. Substance, in this sense, represents all tangible and intangible resources and capabilities within an organization. Organizational culture is that energy which comes from the joint efforts and enthusiastic fulfillment of duties of all employees, and, as a result, adds spark and life to all processes. If the culture is positive and stimulating, then we can expect the desired reaction which results in a superior product and secures growth.

At the same time, we do not want culture to be a counterproductive energy, i.e. an inhibitor, which slows down substance transformation, making resource utilization costly and restricting the organization's growth. In a more rigorous way, there is a fit between strategy and culture which has a direct impact on company performance.

In a positive cultural environment, we become more productive and positively attuned toward colleagues. We speak with enthusiasm to friends about what we do, how important it is, and how good it is to work for our company. If the organization's members are effectively collaborating, positively and naturally attuned toward achieving company goals, this positive energy will aid in creating excellent products even if the materials used are less than perfect. Using culture to generate this level of enthusiasm and commitment is important for any company, established or start-up. Strong culture allows enhanced exploitation of people's competencies, reaching higher behavioral consistency among employees, and overall preparedness for necessary change.

Immortal Soul

A strong soul defines a healthy psychological state and provides strength. If one is going through challenges at a stage when muscles are prepared to give up, the soul pushes forward and thus achieves success. Also, it is important to understand that a company and its culture cannot be separated just as a human being and a soul cannot function independently of each other.

A group of people, even when working toward the same goal, remains a crowd without this intangible, yet vital, element of culture. Culture serves as a force which forms productive and collaborative teams. Culture is born as soon as founders start actively interacting in the creation of a business plan and establishing a new venture, even before the organization is fully formed. They are imprinting the first characteristics of culture, its nature and shape. Unfortunately, the issue of culture is usually a neglected conversation by entrepreneurs and start-up enthusiasts, often at the cost of a slow and ineffective start-up. Entrepreneurs and investors need to look into the cultural properties of a new project as a matter of priority, for in so doing, they will define future growth prospects which can predict future performance.

Spiritual Core

The spiritual core defined by culture is responsible for a sense of belonging, loyalty, pride, and a number of other crucial factors of productive organizational citizenship. Residing in symbols and a proclaimed understanding of the need for effective interaction towards organizational goals, cultural identity in any organization is as unique as human fingerprints and cannot be replicated anywhere else.

When we talk about a person we admire, a common characteristic we note is that this person is able to pull him or herself together when facing difficulties. A person who exhibits such spiritual strength is able to deliver extraordinary performance and reveal inner creativity in the face of adversity.

The same applies in businesses where spiritual identity permeates all operations and processes, forming a solid dome above a company, allowing it to withstand any problem. However, if a company's spiritual identity is weak, it is like being under a leaky shelter, eventually driving its people away.

http://wbp.bz/csa

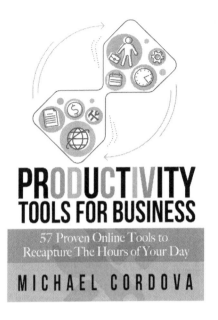
Introduction

"One of the greatest and simplest tools for learning more and growing is doing more." - Washington Irving

In 1993 I founded my software company 21st Century Technologies, Inc. I have since build custom database software systems for the top pharmaceutical and semiconductor companies in the world. Although I still build database software systems, my efforts have moved in the direction of building websites that increase companies sales and doing online marketing, search engine optimization and search engine marketing/pay per click advertising. This experience has led me to founding the publishing company WildBlue Press along with my partner Steve Jackson. I'm past CTO and founder of Mercury Leads along with my partners Paul Plvan and Tom Link, and I'm past CTO of Well.org.

In my marketing shoes I have increased a software product customer's sales from $500,000/year to $4,000,000/year, an 8-fold increase in sales. I increased an HVAC customer's sales by $400K in one month and I have helped countless customers establish, maintain and grow their online presence.

Efficiency and delivery of top-quality services in all of these endeavors is absolutely critical to the success of my companies, and more importantly my customers. I am always on the hunt for great tools that will improve the fruits of my labors and save me time.

In writing this eBook I have literally combed through my installed applications, paid services, daily routines and bookmarks (my bookmark manager is one of the tools) to make sure this list of productivity tools is complete. I have been thinking about doing it for years, now these tools are all here for you to incorporate into your own business and research efforts.

I have no doubt that you will find multiple tools here that will make your life, or the lives of your customers better and more efficient.

Productivity

Use Your Mind Offline

Although this is a technique more than a tool, it is my favorite productivity method to line up my ducks for the time that I make it to my desk for work. I work with many customers for my marketing company, and authors for my publishing company. I do marketing and take care of the websites as well as write books and take care of personal responsibilities. That means I always have a lot of balls that I'm juggling to keep in the air. Many of the tasks I am responsible for are important, if not critical, so I need to make sure they are all completed as required.

What I do to make sure I think of all of the most important tasks - is to get completely away from them all and do something I enjoy that removes me entirely from those very tasks. I find a quiet spot and get back to reading my latest favorite book. While my mind is immersed in the landscapes and characters of the book I'm reading, it is also subconsciously strolling through all that I'm involved in. Periodically a thought will fly by about one of my responsibilities, or maybe (and oftentimes) a great idea. I'll then pull up GMail on my phone or Kindle, make a note to myself and not send the email. I usually have ten or twenty items before I am done reading. When I move on to the rest of my day I send the email and when I'm back at my desk I manage all of this info on my desktop.

Using GMail and my devices is just how I do it. I sync GMail on my devices, so these emails can all be read on all of them. The analog version is to keep a pad of paper and a pen handy.

The biggest benefit of this is that I got some reading done. "I read and think," Warren Buffett once said. "So I do more reading and thinking, and make less impulse decisions than most people in business." (Marguerite Ward, "Warren Buffett's reading routine could make you smarter, science suggests", *http://www.cnbc.com/2016/11/16/warren-buffetts-reading-routine-could-make-you-smarter-suggests-science.html*, November 16, 2016)

Lookout Free Security App for Mobile Devices
https://www.lookout.com

This is the first app you should load onto your smart phone. Available for both the iOS and Android formats this security app performs multiple critical functions for you:

Scans all files and apps you download for viruses
Backs up your contacts
Can locate your device in case you lose it
Has a scream feature that you can invoke remotely

You need to have an account at lookout.com to access your backed up info or find your device after you have lost it. You can also set the device to scream so you can find it. The paid version ($3/month) has Safe Browsing security scans of the web pages you visit in your browser, allows you to lock or wipe the phone remotely and backs up your images.

Team Viewer Free Remote PC Control

https://www.teamviewer.us/

Control your desktop (or any other) pc from any mobile device with this free (for personal use) service. Instead of carrying your laptop everywhere, you can take your iPad or Kindle then access and control your main computer from anywhere. This is a real productivity tool that allows you to do your work immediately anywhere while you are reading your tablet device instead of taking a note and doing the work later.

http://wbp.bz/57toolsa

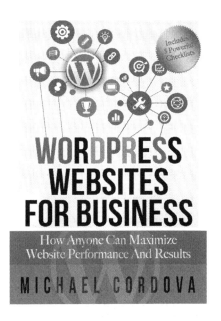
The Importance of Long-Tail Keywords, Intent and the Mobile Factor

When you use keyword phrases consisting of several words in them you have a much better chance of getting ranked for those keyword phrases. Not only that, you can incorporate the users intent in them. For example, let's say you were selling golf clubs. See the following keywords and note how the search terms get more specific and show more intent as you go down:

golf – Someone killing time on their computer

golf clubs – Someone doing general research for golf clubs

pitching wedge – Someone doing general research on pitching wedges

ping G30 driver deals – Someone looking to buy a Ping G30 driver

When doing your keyword research you need to think about what intent you are looking to capture, what specific types of products and services you *want to* provide. Of course it varies by the type of company. Here are some examples of long-tail keywords with intent to engage or purchase:

small business cpa firm to reduce our taxes

auto mechanic to fix my 2017 jeep grand cherokee transmission

chiropractor specializing in a stiff neck

whole roasted pig with green chile catering service (I must be getting hungry)

You need to keep the long-tail and intent concepts in mind when you do your keyword research and write your content. This refinement will make a huge difference in your results. In the above examples, if you instead had focused on cpa firm, auto mechanic, chiropractor or catering service then you'll not only *not be* targeting your company's specific services, but you'll be attempting to rank for keywords that are the most difficult to get top organic rankings for.

Now that we have really smart phones that you can just ask questions of like the Apple Siri or the Android "Ok Google…" capability, and devices like the Amazon Echo (Alexa) and Google Home, search engine queries are now being slanted to those coming from these devices. Now queries like these are becoming more important:

"Ok Google, what's the best Mexican restaurant near me?"

"Alexa, what are the best local activities for kids"

"What are the best local coffee shops"

People are searching on their mobile devices in a hands-free scenario looking for a service that they can use now. *They're on the way!* You need to think about these concepts when you compile your list of keywords that you'll be targeting for your website content.

The Best Tools to Find Long-Tail Keywords

Google again provides great methods and tools to acquire highly relevant long-tail keywords. Since it is Google rankings that you are after, taking Google's suggestions is getting your keywords straight from the horse's mouth.

Do a Google search for your topic and pay attention to the search terms that Google suggests in the search box:

| auto insurance| | 🔍 |

auto insurance
auto insurance **colorado**
auto insurance **quotes**
auto insurance **denver**
auto insurance **florida**
auto insurance **near me**
auto insurance **companies**
auto insurance **america**
auto insurance **comparison**
auto insurance **colorado springs**

Next, scroll down to the bottom of the results of your search and note the other terms (long-tail keywords) that Google suggests for you:

Searches related to concrete contractor

concrete **contractors denver**	**commercial** concrete **contractors denver**
concrete **delivery denver**	**good day** concrete
residential concrete **denver**	**denver** concrete **prices**
denver concrete **services**	**sunny day** concrete

Grab the keyword phrases that are relevant to your current needs and use them in your article. If you need more then recycle - take the relevant ones and use them in another search to get more suggestions.

A favorite tool among marketers is UberSuggest.io. You just type in a seed keyword, and it gives you a ton of other keywords by appending words to your seed keyword starting with each letter of the alphabet. The video at the bottom of the page shows you how to copy and paste these keywords to a spreadsheet and use all of their basic functions.

Another quick source of long-tail keywords is http://soovle.com. Just type in your keyword and they'll list relevant options from Google, Bing, Yahoo!, Wikipedia, Youtube, Answers.com and Amazon.

Many more keyword tools are available in the free download that you can grab from the Resources section at the end of this book.

Use Qualified, Prioritized Keywords to Drive Compelling Content

Once you have completed the above, then you have the information you need to start mapping out your website content. Create a Wordpress category for each of the categories in the spreadsheet. If a category is too broad, then break it down into multiple categories of finer detail. Sort the spreadsheet by two columns - priority then category. This provides you with the keywords most relevant to your business and the topics (categories) that you can provide solutions for. Next create a list of solutions representing a series of posts for each of the categories. You don't have to write the content now, just a list of concepts/solutions that you'll write about. This list will be your content map for future blog posts. Think in terms of problems that your customers are looking to solve, and solutions that you have already provided or can provide.

Ask each member of your team to make a list of the solutions they have provided for customers, then drop each one into the most relevant category. Doing this will provide a great inventory of blog posts that are targeted to solving your customers problems with your company's priorities built-in. They'll be customer-centric in terms of solutions to their problems, and they'll be focusing on keywords that are a priority to your business with a great chance of getting rankings and traffic from them.

This is huge, so if you didn't grasp this concept stop now. Go back and read it again. This is all of the content you'll ever need for your website. As you continue to provide solutions, add more content.

http://wbp.bz/ww4ba

Made in the USA
Lexington, KY
03 September 2019